Who Is the True Seer Driven by God: Balak or Balaam?

Who Is the True Seer Driven by God: Balak or Balaam?

A Text Linguistic and Literary Study of Numbers 22–24

Junhee Lee
FOREWORD BY J. Glen Taylor

WIPF & STOCK · Eugene, Oregon

WHO IS THE TRUE SEER DRIVEN BY GOD: BALAK OR BALAAM?
A Text Linguistic and Literary Study of Numbers 22–24

Copyright © 2022 Junhee Lee. All rights reserved. Except for brief quotations in critical publications or reviews, no part of this book may be reproduced in any manner without prior written permission from the publisher. Write: Permissions, Wipf and Stock Publishers, 199 W. 8th Ave., Suite 3, Eugene, OR 97401.

Wipf & Stock
An Imprint of Wipf and Stock Publishers
199 W. 8th Ave., Suite 3
Eugene, OR 97401

www.wipfandstock.com

PAPERBACK ISBN: 978-1-6667-3603-8
HARDCOVER ISBN: 978-1-6667-9382-6
EBOOK ISBN: 978-1-6667-9383-3

Scripture quotations are from The ESV® Bible (The Holy Bible, English Standard Version®), copyright © 2001 by Crossway, a publishing ministry of Good News Publishers. Used by permission. All rights reserved.

Contents

List of Tables and Diagrams | vii

Foreword | ix

Preface | xi

Acknowledgements | xiii

Abbreviations | xv

Introduction | xvii

Chapter 1: A Survey of Studies on the Balaam Story in Num 22–24 | 1

Chapter 2: Methodology for the Study and Its Application to the Analysis of the Balaam Text of Num 22–24 | 21

Chapter 3: Synthetic Propositions and the Message, Intention, and Theological Implications of the Balaam Story | 114

Conclusion | 129

Bibliography | 131

Author Index | 135

Scripture Index | 137

List of Tables and Diagrams

Table 1. The Occurrences of the Verbal Forms of the Balaam Story | 70
Table 2. Verses Beginning the Sentence without the Vayyiqtol Verb | 71
Table 3. All Verbal Forms in the Balaam Story | 71
Table 4. Verbal Forms of the Seven Poetry Parts in the Balaam Story | 72
Table 5. The Occurrence of the Topical Verb ראה (to See) in the Balaam Story | 73
Table 6. The Occurrence of the Sub-Topical Verbs in the Balaam Story | 75
Table 7. The Occurrence of the Topically-Related Verbs דבר (to Speak), נגד (to Tell), עשׂה (to Do) | 77
Table 8. The Occurrence of the Topically-Related Verb ברך (to Bless) | 79
Table 9. The Occurrence of the Topically-Related Verbs ארר/קבב (to Curse) | 80
Table 10. The Occurrence of the Topically-Related Verbs הרג (to Slay), זבח (to Slaughter), מות (to Die), עלה (to Sacrifice) | 81
Table 11. The Verbal Parallels between the Balaam Story and the Story of Gen 22 | 83
Table 12. The Topical and Sub-Topical Verbs with the Subjects and Objects | 86
Table 13. The Concentric Symmetry Structure of Episodes 1 and 9 | 109
Table 14. The Concentric Symmetry Structure of Episodes 2 and 8 | 109
Table 15. The Concentric Symmetry Structure of Episodes 3 and 7 | 110
Table 16. Verbal Chiasm in Num 22–24 | 122
Diagram 1. The Tensional Relationship among the Main Characters | 111

Foreword

THE REV. DR. JUNHEE Lee's intriguing study of the story of Balak and Balaam in Numbers 22–24 seeks to further our understanding of this important part of the Old Testament by offering four conclusions. First, the narrative characterizes Balaam neither positively nor negatively, but rather as a "neutral" tool of God to deliver a message of blessing to Israel. Second, far from being disparate, the story displays a "topical unity" that unifies parts 1 and 2 of the narrative (chapter 22:2–21 and 22–40). Third, although chapters 22–24 consist of both narrative and individual poems, "topical congruity" provides clarity and coherency. And fourth (and most provocatively), these same chapters have a symmetric shape that consists of nine episodes.
It was a pleasure for me to supervise this challenging study. I commend it particularly as an illustrative example of not only the evident strengths but potential weaknesses inherent to the rigorously consistent application of a narrative and text linguistic approach that seeks to find unity where others have been quick to find it lacking. It is also to be welcomed as a rare and thus important case study in the wider application of a text linguistic method that holds forth promise for better understanding the Old Testament.

J. Glen Taylor, Associate Professor Emeritus of Old Testament and Biblical Proclamation, Wycliffe College, University of Toronto

Preface

THIS MONOGRAPH IS A revised version of my doctoral dissertation, which was submitted in 2019 to the faculty of Knox College (at the University of Toronto) and the biblical department of the Toronto School of Theology. This book focuses on the Balaam story in Num 22–24. Traditional readings of the Balaam story found in Num 22–24 have not provided resolutions to the many textual and hermeneutical problems found in this passage. This deficiency results in the lack of understanding surrounding the purpose of the story. To date, a text linguistic approach has also not been able to decode the passage. Therefore, in this study, I employ a combined text linguistic and literary study of Num 22–24. More specifically, I combine a modified form of Heimerdinger's theory with my own literary approach to the text and argue for the following: (1) that Balaam is a mere tool for delivering God's message; (2) that there is unity between Num 22:2–21 and Num 22:22–40; (3) that topical congruency exists between the prose sections and the poetic collections; and (4) that the purpose of the Balaam story in Num 22–24 is to show God's blessing towards the Israelites.

Acknowledgements

I AM HEARTILY THANKFUL to my supervisor, Dr. Glen Taylor, whose encouragement, guidance, patient support, and careful reading of my work made possible the completion of this dissertation. I also would like to express my deepest gratitude to the members of my committee, Dr. Marion Taylor, Dr. Brian Irwin, Dr. Sarianna Metso, and Dr. Dennis Olson, for their support and encouragement throughout my doctoral studies and dissertation. My special thanks go to ForWord, which is my family-like community. In this community, my family and I were able to go through a long and difficult journey of my study by their prayers and encouragement. I also thank the TaeHwan Kim family for their financial support and prayers. Finally, I am indebted to my loving wife Hyejin Lee and my two children, Elliott and Claire, who embarked with me on a journey of faith, love, and hope during my study. I would not have been able to complete this dissertation without their everlasting love, encouragement, sacrifice, and patience. I also would like to express my heartfelt gratitude to my parents Sangcheol Lee, Sukja Hwang, Yong Hui Kang, and Heung Tae Ko for their unfailing love and supports.

Abbreviations

BDB	Francis Brown, S. R. Driver, and Charles A. Briggs. *Hebrew and English Lexicon of the Old Testament.* Oxford: Clarendon, 1907
BHS	*Biblia Hebraica Stuttgartensia.* Edited by Karl Elliger and Wilhelm Rudolph. Stuttgart: Gesamtherstellun Biblia-Druck, 1977.
BI	*Biblical Interpretation*
ESV	English Standard Version
HALOT	*The Hebrew and Aramaic Lexicon of the Old Testament.* Edited by M. E. J. Richardson. 2 vols. Leiden: Brill, 2001.
JBL	*Journal of Biblical Literature*
JBQ	*Jewish Bible Quarterly*
JSOT	*Journal for the Study of the Old Testament*
JSOTSup	*Journal for the Study of the Old Testament Supplement Series*
MT	Masoretic Text
NASB	New American Standard Bible
NIV	New International Version
SBL	Society of Biblical Literature
SBLSP	*Society of Biblical Literature Seminar Papers.* Edited by G. MacRae. Missoula, MT: Scholars, 1976.
VT	*Vetus Testamentum*

Introduction

Background

PROBLEMS SURROUNDING THE BALAAM story[1] have led to various interpretations.[2] Many scholars focus in on the character of Balaam and are divided on whether Balaam is a prophet of the Lord or a false prophet.[3] Furthermore, historical-critical scholars agree on two important issues when it comes to this text.[4] First, they point out the inconsistency between the account of Balak's calling to Balaam (Num 22:2–20) and the account of Balaam's donkey and the angel (Num 22:21–35). (More specifically, God initially commands Balaam not to go with Balak's officers, but at the end there is a change of mind where he is then allowed to go to Balak.) And, second, they draw attention to the dichotomy between the prose section and the poetic collection in Num 22–24. Regarding this issue, they raise

---

1. There are various titles for the passage of Num 22–24: "the oracle of Balaam" (Bailey, *Leviticus-Numbers*), "Balaam legend" (Knierim and Coats, *Numbers*), "Balaam cycle" (Olson, *Numbers*), "the Balaam pericope" (Levine, *Numbers 21–36*), and "the book of Balaam" (Milgrom, *Numbers*). I prefer "the Balaam story" not for following a specific scholar's theory but for the simple reason that the passage consists of narrations of episodes and plots with mixed prose and poetry sections relating to the character and the role of Balaam.

2. Tosato, "The Literary Structure," 98–106; Notarius, "Poetic Discourse," 55–86; Douglas, *In the Wilderness*, 216–34; Olson, *Numbers*, 140–51; Mann, *The Book of the Torah*, 169–74; Levine, *Numbers 21–36*, 135–276; Van Seters, *The Life of Moses*, 405–35; Knierim and Coats, *Numbers*, 246–63; Milgrom, *Numbers*, 185–210, 467–75; Ashley, *The Book of Numbers*, 432–511.

3. Savelle, "Canonical and Extracanonical Portraits of Balaam," 387–404; Olson, *Numbers*, 140–51; Boyce, *Leviticus and Numbers*, 203–26; Stubbs, *Numbers*, 175–96; Goldingay, *Numbers and Deuteronomy for Everyone*, 56–66; Cole, *Numbers*, 363–432.

4. Noth, *Numbers*, 166–94; Van Seters, *The Life of Moses*, 405–35; Budd, *Numbers*, 248–73; Davies, *Numbers*, 236–84.

INTRODUCTION

some questions such as, "What accounts for the different writing styles between the two parts?" and "Is there thematic coherence between the two sections?"

Traditional studies to date have not provided reasonable answers or solutions to these stated problems and therefore have not been able to answer the question regarding the purpose of this text. Various methodologies have been employed to examine this text, but this study is unique in that, in addition to my own insight, it applies Heimerdinger's theory to the text, using a text linguistic and literary methodology.

Heimerdinger's theory proposes the ability to make clear the implied author's intention[5] or purpose behind Hebrew narratives of the Old Testament.[6] His text linguistic theory and my own literary study, then, can be

---

5. The term "the implied author's intention" in my dissertation is close to the concept of it in New Criticism. This new revolution shifted the interpretive key from the author to the text. New Critics insist that the text is an organic whole, an autonomous, self-sufficient, and objective work that needs to be examined on its own terms. Therefore, they emphasize the text over the role of the author and the reader. New Critics ruled out the concerns of the author because they are cautious about the intentional fallacy (the design or intention of the author is neither available nor desirable as a standard for judging the success of a work of literary art). The fallacy, according to its proponents, claims that it is wrong to regard the intention of the author as a standard in judging the text's meaning and worth. However, for the New Critics, the intention of the author cannot define the meaning of a work of art. Once the text is produced by the author, it has a self-contained and closed narrative world which is not controlled by the author. The meaning of the text must be public and objective. Thus the meaning need not be equivalent to the author's intention. Meaning lies within the work of literature itself and it can surpass the intentions of the historical author.

Booth, in his book *A Rhetoric of Irony* (11), invented the term "implied author." According to him, "It is true that the author I am interested in is only the creative person responsible for the choices that made the work—what I have elsewhere called the 'implied author' who is found in the work itself." He suggests that "the details of our reconstruction will depend, of course, on how our knowledge and experience relate to the implied author's intention . . . The decision about which side of the line we are on is once again a decision about the total intention of the author implied by the work" (147, 242). This hypothetical person is a second self or an official scribe who is created by the narrative world. Thus in the narrative there is an implied author. It is important to know the rhetorical devices by which the implied author expresses and communicates his worldview to the implied reader. The implied reader is brought to see how the implied author evaluates or perceives the events, characters, and settings in the narrative.

In conclusion, when I use the term "implied author's intention," I don't mean the intention of the historical author, but the implied author's intention which is equivalent to the meaning of the text by the implied author in my dissertation.

6. Here, in the concept of author's intention, "author" can be defined as a narrator rather than an author who contains a historical context.

INTRODUCTION

applied to the proposed text to examine the purpose of the Balaam story, as well as to suggest the solution to the arguments above: (1) the role of Balaam; (2) the unity between Num 22:2–20 and Num 22:21–35; (3) the topical congruency between the prose section and the poetic collection; and (4) the purpose of the Balaam story as a whole.

The Balaam story has attracted the attention of biblical scholars who employ a variety of approaches. Some scholars have thus shown interest in the writing styles within the story. For example, Notarius examined the issue of poetic discourse and verbal tenses in the oracles of Balaam,[7] whereas Tosato studied the literary structure of the poems of Balaam.[8] Other scholars have focused in on the character of Balaam. Douglas, for example, regarded the story of Balaam as a play within a play that served to convey a political satire that critiqued life at the time.[9] Olson regarded the Balaam story as one of at least three texts, such as the spy story (Num 13–14), the Balaam story (Num 22–24), and some laws (Num 15, 27, and 36) that highlight God's blessing on his people, especially the new generation of Israel in the wilderness. For him, "the story of Balaam occupies a strategic position at the end of the first generation and before the genesis of a new generation."[10] "Through the mouth of a foreign prophet, God blesses Israel with accolades and promises that are unsurpassed in the rest of the Pentateuch."[11] Olson's interest in the Balaam story is in regards to the role or character of Balaam in the theology of Numbers. Mann reads the Balaam story as a power game between Yahweh, who is the God of Israel, and Balaam who is a pagan diviner.[12] He is interested in the character of Balaam, with his international reputation and the tension between Yahweh and Balaam around the issue of blessing and curse toward the people of Israel, even though Balaam turned to bless Israel later.[13] Levine focuses on the character of Balaam in the Balaam story and comments that "the bulk of Num 22–24 centers around the figure of Balaam and consists of narratives and poems."[14] He also introduced the Deir 'Allā inscription, which is

---

7. Notarius, "Poetic Discourse," 55–86.
8. Tosato, "The Literary Structure," 98–106.
9. Douglas, *In the Wilderness*, 216–34.
10. Olson, *Numbers*, 151.
11. Olson, *Numbers*, 140–42.
12. Mann, *The Book of the Torah*, 136.
13. Mann, *The Book of the Torah*, 136–40.
14 Levine, *Numbers 21–36*, 137–38.

Introduction

equivalent to the Balaam story in Num 22–24, to provide a historical *Sitz im Leben* of the Balaam text.[15]

Still other scholars have undertaken form-critical and source-critical studies on the text. Van Seters examined the story of Balaam on the basis of the documentary hypothesis and continued his discussion on the issues of "the prose and the poetic oracles within the broader comparative context and the tradition history of the Balaam tradition generally."[16] Knierim and Coats dealt with the Balaam story as serving "the Yahwistic source as a key for the divine appointment of kingship for Israel/Jacob."[17] For him, the blessing from Yahweh toward Israel is the Yahwistic expression for the victory and intimacy that Yahweh possesses for his people Israel.

Further, Milgrom, who includes Rabbinic tradition, claims that "the Balaam story was composed independently and later inserted into the Pentateuchal corpus."[18] He also examines the unity of the story, the episode of the ass, the character of Balaam, the profession of Balaam, and the Balaam inscription.

Finally, Ashley and other scholars have discussed literary and theological aspects of the Balaam story. But Ashley uniquely suggests that "the text of chs. 22–24 is not concerned to pronounce on the character of Balaam. Balaam's character is incidental to the story."[19]

Methodology

My methodology involves the analysis of the text from a text linguistic and literary perspective for the purpose of identifying and arguing for unity in this story. The more exegetically nuanced theory of Heimerdinger in the area of text linguistics lays the foundation for research regarding the meaning of the text in this narrative, and further provides clarity on the relationship between the prose and poetic sections. Adapting Heimerdinger's theory, I will apply it to the large unit of text found in the Balaam story.

---

15. Levine, *Numbers 21–36*, 230–34; cf. Cole, *Numbers*, 367–70; Ashley, *The Book of Numbers*, 437–40; Milgrom, *Numbers*, 473–76; Dozeman, "The Book of Numbers," 2:178. I will introduce the Deir 'Allā inscription and its relevance to the Balaam narrative in chapter 1 in detail.

16. Van Seters, *The Life of Moses*, 405.

17. Knierim and Coats, *Numbers*, 246–62.

18. Milgrom, *Numbers*, 185.

19. Ashley, *The Book of Numbers*, 435.

Introduction

This study will primarily make use of, but not be completely restricted to, a text linguistic and literary approach to interpret the text for the purposes of understanding the implied author's intention, particularly as it relates to the textual questions and problems identified in this text. This modified text linguistic theory of Heimerdinger will be used together with my own literary approach.

First, it is necessary to introduce the concepts of topic, focus and foregrounding according to Heimerdinger and another scholar. Buth approached the issue of subject and topic from the perspective of the generative syntactic movement. According to him, a topic, pragmatically, is "a specially signaled constituent for the purposes of relating the clause to the larger context"[20]; "topic" and "subject" are thus synonymous. For Buth, "focus refers to a specially signaled constituent for highlighting salient information of a clause. This information may be contrastive. It may be contra-expected, that is, the speaker/writer assumes his or her audience may be expecting something different and so marks it for focus. It may also be new information that is specially marked to fill in, or to complete, assumed missing information. It may also be old information that needs special reinforcement through repetition."[21]

Heimerdinger defines "topic" as "the starting point of an utterance . . . a term to describe what a text is all about; its subject matter."[22] He suggests that the important issues of topic continuity and topic should be the center of attention. He also, importantly, introduces "topicality, which is best described cognitively as the centering of attention of a speaker and hearer upon discourse entities which are the main concern of the story."[23] It is important that Heimerdinger, when dealing with the issue of speaker-hearer, considers topicality to be his pivotal point in his discussion of topic, focus, and foreground. This is the case because it shows that his theory and insights are very applicable to an exegetical study, and specifically to a literary interpretation of a text in which a reader (hearer) is interested in the implied intention of an author/narrator (speaker). In my investigation I will address topicality, since it is extremely important for this study. Regarding focus, Heimerdinger defines it as "the most important piece

---

20. Buth, "Word Order in the Verbless Clause," 81.
21. Buth, "Word Order in the Verbless Clause," 81.
22. Heimerdinger, *Topic, Focus and Foreground*, 101–02.
23. Heimerdinger, *Topic, Focus and Foreground*, 123–25.

Introduction

of new information mentioned by the speaker."[24] Regarding the issue of foregrounding, Heimerdinger insists that foregrounding is not a concept that should be understood in terms of a dichotomous relationship between foreground and background. Rather, according to Heimerdinger, foregrounding functions to grab the attention of the reader of the narrative through markers such as unexpectedness and internal/external evaluation of the author or narrator.[25]

Second, it is important to note that the verb ראה (to see) functions as the topic/theme of the Balaam story. This verb occurs not only in the very first sentence, but then throughout the narrative in pivotal points of the story. This observation will play an important role in my literary approach and investigation of the Balaam story.

In applying Heimerdinger's theory to the text of Num 22–24, I will argue that there is present a controlling topicality which indicates a consistency throughout the whole narrative. Moreover, I will show that the development of the topicality discloses the meaning of the text, and that the story is well-organized to communicate its intended message because of the cooperation between the topical, sub-topical, and topically-related verbs. According to the theory of Heimerdinger, topicality begins with the heading of a narrative, and the heading consists of information such as action, character, and location. In modification and contrast to the theory of Heimerdinger, I would like to argue that the action (verb) is the most influential topical element that controls the flow of a narrative, and that the combination of verb (topical) + character provides effective understanding of the topicality in a text.

I believe that the Balaam story indicates that the God of Israel himself hires a foreign diviner, Balaam, to deliver the message of blessing to the Israelites. In the course of the story, we see that the actions of God prevent Balak from seeing what he wishes regarding the fate of the Israelites—he

---

24. Heimerdinger, *Topic, Focus and Foreground*, 163.

25. Heimerdinger, *Topic, Focus and Foreground*, 222–24. He quotes Dry, such as "foregrounding is defined in terms of salience." According to him, "Given the implicit and agreed norm, do not make your contribution more informative than is required; a deviation from this principle will be felt by the hearer or reader to be significant and a deviating element which creates an overloading of information will be perceived as salient. Foregrounding may thus be obtained through the violation of the norms of normal communication." He insists that "In Old Hebrew narratives, the information principle is mainly flouted by repetitions of words, phrases, or sentences . . . The second foregrounding mechanism is based on the unexpectedness or unpredictability of an element in context."

Introduction

wished to see the Israelites cursed. God accomplishes this by making Balaam see the angel of God first. Then, by allowing Balaam to see the Israelites, he blesses the Israelites, who ultimately reveal the supreme power of God who controls his people and other nations and leads his people to the promised land. The topicality of ראה (to see), accompanied by Balaam's mission, where he functions as God's tool, maximizes the dramatic aspect of the blessing message to the Israelites. The topicality of ראה (to see) in the sense of God's blessing and the action of ראה (to see) extends the topicality in cooperation with other sub-topical and topically-related verbs in the whole Balaam story. In this well-organized story there is absent any specific comment concerning the character of Balaam, whether he is a true diviner or false prophet. Moreover, I will also argue that there is no evidence to indicate that what we have in this narrative are traces of two inconsistent blocks of material that are derived from two contrasting sources. In addition, I will also argue for the presence of coherence and thematic connection between the prose section and poetic sections, which is indicated by common topicality.

Procedure

In chapter 1, I will introduce some previous studies that have considered the Balaam story of Num 22–24. More specifically, I will show the concerns of previous studies on the Balaam story of Num 22–24. The first approach argues for Balaam's character: positive, negative, and neutral evaluations of the character of Balaam. The second is the studies on the features of the narrative and the oracles in the Balaam story. Lastly, there are studies on the relationship between the prose and poetic sections of the Balaam story. In this chapter I will review the various viewpoints on the story of Balaam.

Chapter 2 will proceed with my methodology for the study and its application to the analysis of the Balaam text of Num 22–24. In the part of methodology, I will discuss mainly the concept of topicality, the importance of verb, the topical verbs, and the development of topicality in a text. In the part on analysis of the text, I will present the analyzed Hebrew and English texts of Num 22–24 and discuss the topical, sub-topical, and topically-related verbs, the composition of the Balaam text according to sections and episodes, and the structures of the Balaam story.

The purpose of this chapter is to apply my methodology to the exegetical problems of the text. I will therefore show the process of the application

Introduction

and necessary discussions to disclose the meaning of the text concerning the story of Balaam. I believe that the whole picture of the Balaam story can be revealed through the use of topicality. It is through the whole picture and the details of the story that one is enabled to understand the purpose of the story of Balaam. Pursuing the meaning of the text is important, since it is the key to solving the given textual issues that have been stated above.

Chapter 3 will consist of the conclusions derived from the study along with its theological implications. In this chapter there will be a summary of the proposed studies on the following topics: (1) how the study reveals the role of Balaam, (2) how it determines unity between Num 22:2–21 and 22:22–40, (3) how it shows topical congruency between the prose section and the poetic collection, and, finally, (4) the message, intention, and theological implications concerning how it demonstrates the purpose of the Balaam story in Num 22–24.

Chapter 1

A Survey of Studies on the Balaam Story in Num 22–24

Introduction

SCHOLARLY INTEREST IN THE book of Numbers since the 1900s has been dominated by particular interest in the Balaam story in Num 22–24.[1] This disproportionate interest may be due to its odd form as well as the narrative itself. Consisting of both prose and poetry, these chapters narrate the experience of the foreigner Balaam's direct interaction with the God of Israel when he is called upon by Balak, the king of Moab, to curse the Israelites. The bizarre sequence of events, including Balaam's interaction with his talking donkey, have drawn out numerous interpretations.

My scholarly questions about this text are fourfold. First, what is the role of Balaam in the narrative? Second, how does the narrative of Num 22:2–21 relate to the narrative of Num 22:22–35? Third, what is the

---

1. Yahuda, "The Name of Balaam's Homeland," 547–51; Zannoni, "Balaam: International Seer / Wizard Prophet," 5–19; Tosato, "The Literary Structure," 98–106; Coats, "The Way of Obedience," 53–79; Baskin, "Origen on Balaam," 22–35; Safren, "Balaam and Abraham," 105–13; Moore, *The Balaam Traditions*, 1–123; Greene, *Balaam and His Interpreters*, 1–169; Layton, "Whence Comes Balaam," 32–61; Savran, "Beastly Speech," 33–55; Dijkstra, "The Geography of the Story of Balaam," 72–97; Dijkstra, "Is Balaam Also among the Prophets?" 43–64; Lutzky, "Ambivalence toward Balaam," 421–25; Douglas, *In the Wilderness*, 216–34; Alter, "Balaam and the Ass," 6–32; Begg, "Balaam's Talking Ass," 207–28; Notarius, "Poetic Discourse," 55–86; Sals, "The Hybrid Story of Balaam," 315–35; Moyer, "Literary and Linguistic Studies in Sefer Bil'am (Numbers 22–24)," 1–550; Way, "Animals in the Prophetic World," 47–62; Albright, "The Oracles of Balaam," 207–33; Moyer, "Who Is the Prophet, and Who the Ass?" 167–83; Spero, "Moses Wrote His Book and the Portion of Balaam," 193–200.

relationship between prose and poetry in the Balaam story in Num 22–24? Fourth, what is the intention of the Balaam story in Num 22–24?

Traditional readings of the Balaam story found in Num 22–24 have not provided adequate resolutions to the many textual and hermeneutical problems inherent in answering these questions. This deficiency results in the lack of understanding surrounding the purpose of the story. To date, a text linguistic approach has also not been able to decode the passage. Therefore, in this study, I will employ a combined text linguistic and literary study of Num 22–24. More specifically, I will combine a modified form of Heimerdinger's theory with my own literary approach to the text and argue for the following: (1) that Balaam is a mere tool for delivering God's message; (2) that there is unity between Num 22:2–20 and Num 22:21–35; (3) that topical congruency exists between the prose section and the poetic collection; and (4) that the purpose of the Balaam story in Num 22–24 is to show God's blessing towards the Israelites.

However, it is necessary to briefly mention other studies showing the traditional discussions by scholars on the Balaam text outside of the areas that I have focused on in my research. Scholars have various interests in the text of the Balaam story. Amongst them, concerns regarding source criticism and the Deir 'Allā inscription are prominent.[3]

---

2. Ashley, *The Book of Numbers*, 434. Some scholars, such as Ashley, suggest that the independent Balaam story begins at Num 22:2. I also insist that the literary unit of the Balaam story begins at Num 22:2.

3. Besides source criticism and the Deir 'Allā inscription, there is also interest in the texts of the Dead Sea Scrolls regarding the Balaam text in Num 22–24: Leviticus-Numbersa and 4QNumb. Cf. García Martínez and Tigchelaar, *The Dead Sea Scrolls Study Edition*, 252; Tov, "A Didactic Approach to the Biblical Dead Sea Scrolls," 184, 194; Abegg et al., *The Dead Sea Scrolls Bible*, 108–09, 125–29. In Numbers 22–24 from scroll 4Q23 Leviticus-Numbersa, there are no new words in the scroll that are not in the traditional text. Comparatively, in Numbers 22–24 from scroll 4Q27Numbersb, there are new words which are in the scroll, but not in the traditional text: "and they are dwelling next to me" (in 22:11), "And the princes of Moab stayed with Balaam" (in 22:19), "And Balak went and stood by his burnt offering and Balaam called to God" (in 23:3), and "against Jacob or omens against Israel" (in 24:1). However, these different words from 4QNumb do not affect the meaning from the MT. Nonetheless, Abegg et al, *The Dead Sea Scrolls Bible*, 108–09, introduce the important position of 4QNumb as follows: "The third special Numbers scroll is 4QNumb, which is by far the best preserved and contains material from chapters 11–36. This manuscript may be described as an early Jewish 'living Bible,' since it features many interpolations of other material and expansions of the biblical text . . . Many of the longer readings included in 4QNumb are not found in the Masoretic Text and the Septuagint but are often preserved in the Samaritan Pentateuch. To a lesser extent, 4QNumb also contains readings present in the Greek Bible but not in

Notably, some scholars and discussions engage the sources such as J, E, and JE with respect to the Balaam story in Num 22–24.[4] Gray insists that "most writers, therefore, are now agreed that the present narrative is a compilation from the two sources J and E."[5] He argues that the distribution of the two divine names can verify the dependence of the Balaam story on J and E.

Noth insists that the Balaam story is an old narrative in the Pentateuch and that the story does not show unity.[6] According to him, there is indisputable evidence that the Balaam story utilized J and E as sources. He points out that the narrative of the donkey (22:21–35) belongs to the J-narrative, and that the sections comprised of 22:41–23:26 and 23:28–24:19 are representatives of E and J sources respectively.[7] But, he also insists that the divine designations ("Yahweh" and "Elohim") are used too inconsistently to be employed to differentiate the sources in the text of Num 22–24. However, Noth offers very few explanations for his conjectures, and he simply concludes that the Balaam narrative intends to show a foreigner acknowledging and confessing Yahweh, the God of Israel.[8]

Against the use of source criticism in Num 22–24, Dijkstra insists that "the classical division of the text in Jahwistic and Elohistic components has basically been given up because the alternative use of the divine names YHWH and Elohim cannot be explained in a satisfactory way by source-criticism."[9] Dozeman also insists that "the distribution of the divine names in these chapters is, indeed, striking. But an overview indicates that their use is for literary and theological reasons, and not the result of a history of

---

the Masoretic Text or Samaritan Pentateuch . . . Since 4QNumb is one example of these 'different' textual forms, it gives us a precious window on one textual tradition that differs markedly from the Hebrew Bible and English translations that are used today."

4. Gray, *A Critical and Exegetical Commentary on Numbers*, 309; Noth, *Numbers*, 171; Greene, *Balaam and His Interpreters*, 16–68; Van Seters, *The Life of Moses*, 405–35; Van Seters, "From Faithful Prophet to Villain," 126–32; Campbell and O'Brien, *Sources of the Pentateuch*, 87, 157–59, 191–93. Campbell and O'Brien suggest that Num 22:1b is from the priestly source.

5. Gray, *A Critical and Exegetical Commentary on Numbers*, 309.

6. Noth, *Numbers*, 171.

7. Noth, *Numbers*, 171–72.

8. Noth, *Numbers*, 174.

9. Dijkstra, "The Geography of the Story of Balaam," 73; Albright, "The Oracles of Balaam," 207–08.

composition."¹⁰ Levine also insists that there is not enough evidence for the documentary sources in the Balaam story because the divine names appear in mixed and irregular manner in the story.¹¹ Ashley insists that "stylistic reasons" caused the occurrence of the various divine names.¹² For him, the text of the Balaam story must be interpreted in its final form rather in light of the sources behind the text.¹³

I agree with the aforementioned scholars that the criterion of divine names is not a reliable criterion for discerning sources in this material, and will therefore not invoke the source critical designations of J, E, JE, or P in considering this material. Indeed, the practice of some to classify each individual verse into J, E, or JE strikes many contemporary scholars as highly conjectural and disregardful (or ignorant of) broader considerations that support literary cohesiveness.

In terms of the status of Pentateuchal scholarship as it relates to Numbers and as is reflected in the most recent scholarship, Frevel's summary is succinct and helpful:

> (1) The challenge of the European consensus in terms of the end of the P narrative in current source-critical scholarship.
>
> (2) The dissent with regard to the existence and extent of Holiness School material in Numbers, taking into account the wider background of different concepts of how H and P materials generally relate in the Pentateuch.
>
> (3) The challenge of a pre-priestly continuation of theeExodus narrative in the wilderness in some influential parts of present-day scholarship.
>
> (4) The increased interest in the formation of the Torah in the Persian period and its relation to religious, social, and political developments in the Second Temple period.¹⁴

---

10. Dozeman, "The Book of Numbers," 2:180. It is more persuasive that the phenomenon of the occurrences of the various divine names is not because of the different sources behind the text but because of the author's linguistic choices, even though it is not easy to decide the reason for employing specific names in the text.

11. Levine, *Numbers 21–36*, 137–38.

12. Ashley, *The Book of Numbers*, 434.

13. Ashley, *The Book of Numbers*, 433.

14. Frevel, "The Book of Numbers," 6.

Frevel raises a question concerning why the role of Numbers is crucial based on his interests in priestly traditions, post-priestly additions and redactions as the core of the composition history of Numbers. According to him, "the so-called priestly and post-priestly texts in the book of Numbers" exist, and "the priestly 'strata' in Numbers relate to each other ... [and] to the non-priestly layers (e.g., the killing of Balaam, Num 31:8 to Num 22–24)."[15] In his introductory article, Frevel mentions Num 22–24 in the interest of source criticism, such as the priestly source or non-priestly source, and redaction, such as the priestly strata or the non-priestly layers. However, he does not seem to treat the text of Num 22–24 to develop his foundational interest in redaction criticism.

In the same book, *Torah and the Book of Numbers*, Robker examined Num 22–24 based on his interest in redactional history.[16] His examination on Num 22–24 leads to the following conclusion:

> To summarize the findings thus far: 22:2 seems to be from a different author or redactor than 22:1 and 3b, and all of these verses appear to be later than 22:3a and 4. The elders of Midian in 22:4 and 7 (and possibly the rest of 7a) were probably secondarily introduced into the present narrative context. The story of Balaam's donkey in 22:21–35a represents a secondary insertion into the primary story and may have been included to tarnish Balaam's otherwise positive appearance. Similarly, 23:4b may have been added into the original composition in order to tarnish Balaam's reputation, though this is more uncertain. Finally, it is likely that the fourth oracle in 24:14b–24 or some portion(s) of it were added at a later stage or stages.[17]

Robker suggests that "beyond these minor insertions and additions, there is no need to postulate multiple sources behind the Balaam narrative as has been done in various permutations of the Documentary Hypothesis."[18] However, similar to the practice of source criticism (J, E, or JE in the Balaam

---

15. Frevel, "The Book of Numbers," 31–32.

16. Robker, "The Balaam Narrative," 334. "It will be demonstrated that the Balaam narrative probably existed as an independent literary unit before its incorporation into a larger contiguous pre-Deuteronomistic narrative that was expanded on at least one more occasion. The development of the Balaam narrative in Numbers generally parallels the development of the Balaam tradition found in other biblical texts."

17. Robker, "The Balaam Narrative," 344.

18. Robker, "The Balaam Narrative," 344.

text), the redactional examination of Robker on Num 22–24 also seems to reduce the text into fragments without strong evidence.

On the other hand, many scholars are interested in the study of the Balaam story in the light of the texts from the Deir 'Allā inscription.[19] Levine presents the translation of Combination I in the Deir 'Allā inscription as follows:[20]

1. The misfortunes of the book of Balaam, the son of Beor; a divine seer is he.
2. Then the gods came (to him) at night, and he beheld a vision in accordance with El's utterance.
3. They said to Balaam, son of Beor:
4. "So will be done, with naught surviving;
5. "No one has seen [the likes of] what you have heard!"
6. Balaam arose on the morrow, behold [ ]
7. He summoned *the heads of the assembly* unto him,
8. And for two days he fasted, and wept bitterly.
9. Then his intimates entered into his presence, and they said to Balaam, the son of Beor:
10. "Why do you fast, and why do you weep?"
11. Then he said to them:
12. "Be seated, and I will tell you what the Shadday-gods have planed,
13. "And go, see the acts of the gods!
14. "The gods have banded together, and the Shadday-gods have established a council.

---

19. Levine, *Numbers 21–36*, 241–75; Cole, *Numbers*, 367–70; Ashley, *The Book of Numbers*, 437–40; Milgrom, *Numbers*, 473–76; Dozeman, "The Book of Numbers," 2:178. Dozemann notes that "the Deir 'Allā text provides two starting points for interpreting Numbers 22–24. First, the role of Balaam in Numbers 22–24 arises from Israel's larger cultural context, where the character had achieved legendary significance as a diviner by the eighth century BC. Second, Balaam appears to be a positive character in the Deir 'Allā text rather than a negative or sinister diviner." See also: Levine, *Numbers 21–36*, 230–34; cf. Van Seters, *The Life of Moses*, 407–13; Greene, *Balaam and His Interpreters*, 2–5; Moore, *The Balaam Traditions*, 7–9, 66–96.

20. I introduce only Combination I because Combination I is more reliable than Combination II regarding the information of Balaam. Cf. Moore, *The Balaam Traditions*, 8. According to Moore, "Interpretation of DAT II, however, remains problematic. The text is more fragmentary here than in DAT I:1–7, and Balaam's name cannot be found on Combination II at all. Still, for epigraphical, paleographical, philological, and other reasons which will be elaborated below, few scholars believe that Combination II should be separated from Combination I."

15. "And they have said to [the goddess] Shagar:
16. 'Sew up, close up the heavens with dense cloud,
17. 'That darkness exist there, not brilliance, *Obscurity and not clarity*;
18. 'So that you instill dread in dense darkness.
19. 'And never utter a sound again!'
20. "It shall be that the swift and crane will shriek insult to the eagle,
21. "And a nest of vultures shall cry out in response.
22. "The stork, the young of the falcon and the owl,
23. "The chicks of the heron, sparrow, and cluster of eagles;
24. "Pigeons and birds, [and fowl in the s]ky.
25. "And a rod shall [flay the cat]tle; where there are ewes, a staff shall be brought.
26. "Hares—eat together!
27. "Free[ly feed,] oh the beasts [of the field]!
28. "And [freely] drink, asses and hyenas!"
29. Heed the admonition, adversaries of Sha[gar-and-Ishtar]!
30. [   ] skilled diviner.
31. To skilled diviners one shall take you, and to an oracle, [to] a perfumer of myrrh and a priestess.
32. [Who] *covers his body* [with oil], *and rubs himself with olive oil.*
33. To one bearing an offering in a horn; one augurer after another, and yet another.
34. One augurer broke away *from his colleagues*;
35. And the striking force departed [ ]
36. And they heard incantations from afar.
37. [   ]
38. Then disease was unleashed [   ], and all beheld acts of distress.
39. Shagar-and-Ishtar did not [ ]
40. The piglet [drove out] the leopard;
41. And the [   ] drove out the young of [the   ].
42. [   ] double offerings.
43. And he beheld—[21]

---

21. Levine, *Numbers 21–36*, 245–46.

Who Is the True Seer Driven by God?

According to Cole, the texts of the Deir 'Allā inscription, which were excavated at the plain of the Jordan River Valley, have been dated in the eighth or seventh century BC.[22] The inscription, which was written in an Aramaic-like dialect, narrates the events regarding Balaam, son of Beor. Cole summarizes the contents of the inscription as follows:

> One Balaam son of Beor, who is described as a "seer of the gods," had a frightening night vision that he shared with his colleagues in the midst of his fasting and grief. He foretells a period of drought and darkness, of mourning and death, and in which the natural order is upended. Small birds like the swift and the sparrow attack larger ones like the eagle and the pigeon; the deaf hear at a distance, and fools have insightful visions. Balaam then perhaps exercises his prophetic-divination expertise to confront or curse the gods and goddesses who have brought on this calamity, and he implores the goddesses Ashtar (consort of Chemosh in Moab) and Sheger (known from Ugarit and Phoenician sources) to bring light, rain, and fertility to the land.[23]

Comparison between the Balaam story in Num 22–24 and the Balaam texts of the Deir 'Allā inscription (from my examination on Levine's translation and Cole's summary of Combination I in the Deir 'Allā inscription) discloses several differences between the two:

1. Biblical Balaam does not have a title, while extrabiblical Balaam has the title of "a divine seer."
2. Biblical Balaam is dependent on the Lord, while the extrabiblical Balaam is able to see a vision in accordance with El's utterance as a representative of his colleagues.
3. The oracles reveal the will of the Lord toward his people in the Balaam story in Num 22–24, while the Balaam texts of Deir 'Allā relate to mostly natural phenomena.
4. There is unfolding of tension between the Lord, Balaam, and Balak in the Balaam story in Num 22–24, while, through the commission of gods, Balaam has distress (he fasts and weeps) because of disease on behalf of his people in the Balaam texts of the Deir 'Allā inscription.[24]

---

22. Cole, *Numbers*, 367.
23. Cole, *Numbers*, 368.
24. Moore, *The Balaam Traditions*, 8. "Nevertheless, at present there does appear to be some basic agreement with regard to the gist of Combination I (particularly lines 1–7,

5. The Balaam story in Num 22–24 reveals the everlasting will and grace of the Lord toward his people, while the Balaam text of the Deir ʿAllā inscription is interested in the disease from the gods.[25]

Based on these differences, we may conclude that the Balaam story in Num 22–24 has little to do with the Balaam texts of Deir ʿAllā inscription regarding the contents and message of the former. The examination of the inscription does, however, allow us to confirm some information, as summarized by Ashley: (1) "Balaam . . . was a known literary character in the Transjordan"; (2) "the social and religious roles of Balaam as both a diviner/seer (*bārû*) and an exorcist (*ašipu*) in both Balaam cycles" are similar; and (3) "the divine names used in the Deir ʿAllā Balaam texts and the biblical texts are similar."[26]

Now, I would like to survey the studies on the Balaam story in Num 22–24 regarding the issues that I suggested above are relevant to this study; (1) whether the purpose of the Balaam story in Num 22–24 is to pass judgment on the character of Balaam; (2) how does the narrative of Num 22:2–21 relate to the narrative of Num 22:22–35?; (3) the relationship between prose and poetry in the Balaam story in Num 22–24; (4) the intention of the Balaam story in Num 22–24. This introduction will refer to the discussions of Gray, Noth, Budd, Milgrom, Ashley, Olson, Levine, and Wenham primarily, and include other scholars' insights on related issues when necessary.[27]

---

because there is more text to work with here than anywhere else). This tradition shows us a fairly typical divine council, composed of beings called *'lhn* ('gods') who commission a 'seer' (*ḥzh*) named Balaam bar Beor to communicate an ominous message to 'his people' (*ʿmh*)."

25. Greene, *Balaam and His Interpreters*, 4. "He [Balaam] is frightened by its contents, for his people are to be chastised by fire as punishment for somehow having rebelled against their gods."

26. Ashley, *The Book of Numbers*, 439–40.

27. Cf. Lee, *Punishment and Forgiveness*, 5. I basically agree with the scholars' list that Lee suggested in his profound study of Numbers. Although the Lee's list was made in the interest of the structural study in the book of Numbers, the scholars in the list show their exhaustive and insightful argumentations in the whole book of Numbers as well as various issues of the Balaam story. Therefore, I selected some scholars from Lee's list for this study. According to Lee, *Punishment and Forgiveness*, 5, "Gray depends on literary-critical distinctions; Noth and Budd are based on tradition-historical criticism interested in the history of the literary growth of the text; others deal with the text in its present or final form." By "others" Lee includes, in addition to the first six scholars I mention above, Maier and Davies, whom I do not consider. Levine's two-volume work

Who Is the True Seer Driven by God?

Studies on Balaam's Character

Evaluations of Balaam's character as presented in both Testaments and by extrabiblical readers can be divided into three positions: positive, negative, and neutral.[28] Modern scholars positively evaluating Balaam's character mostly base their conclusions on the text of Num 22–24.[29] Of the biblical passages that evaluate Balaam's character negatively, OT passages such as Num 31:16, Deut 23:3–6, and Josh 24:9–10 do not refer to the obvious evil conduct of Balaam, while NT passages such as 2 Pet 2:15–16, Jude 11, and Rev 2:14 mention the specific points of his wrongdoings in detail and negatively evaluate the traditions of Moab, Balak's homeland. Passages including Mic 6:5 and Neh 13:2 neutrally evaluate Balaam's character.

Why do the various passages of both Testaments respond differently to the original text of Num 22–24? In what follows, I will further analyze the three categories of assessments of Balaam's character, positive, negative, and neutral, respectively.

Positive Evaluations of the Character of Balaam

Noth argues for the priority of the text in Num 22–24 among the many Balaam traditions. Noth rightly insists that the Balaam tradition in Num 22–24 is "the oldest literary form of the Balaam tradition and the only primary one," and the negative images of Balaam in Num 31, Rev 2:14, 2 Pet 2:15, and Jude 11 came from other secondary and later traditions of Balaam.[30] According to Noth, the original text of the Balaam story, Num 22–24, should be given exegetical priority among many Balaam traditions. Noth puts forth several reasons to evaluate Balaam's character positively.

---

considers the book of Numbers sometimes chapter by chapter and at other times, such as Num 22–24, by section. Wenham's credible discussion of Numbers also deals with macro and integrated subjects as well.

28. The primary passage reflecting a positive evaluation on Balaam is Mic 6:5 (cf. Way, "Animals in the Prophetic World," 51). Passages reflecting a negative evaluation on Balaam include Num 31:8, 16; Deut 23:3–6; Josh 13:22, 24:9–10; 2 Pet 2:15–16; Jude 11; and Rev 2:14. Neutral evaluations of Balaam are found in Num 31:8; Josh 13:22; Neh 13:1–2; and Mic 6:5. See Savelle, "Canonical and Extracanonical Portraits of Balaam," 387–404, for various canonical and extracanonical evaluations of Balaam.

29. Gray, *Numbers*, 315–21. Although Gray mentions that Balaam's character is not the primary interest of the writer of the story, he evaluates Balaam's character positively. Cf. Budd, *Numbers*, 261–65; Olson, *Numbers*, 140–51.

30. Noth, *Numbers*, 173.

First, Balaam went to Balak with Yahweh's permission. Second, "the theme of coming to bless instead of to curse is certainly the primary one."[31] Finally, "the purpose of the narrative from the very beginning was, without doubt, the recording of the blessings of the famous Balaam."[32]

Budd contends for the positive character of Balaam through his examination of J and E sources.[33] According to Budd, Balaam is described as a true prophet: "Not only is he sensitive to Yahweh's word, but he also recognizes Yahweh as *his* God (22:18)."[34] Balaam "refuses to be enticed into faithlessness by the promise of wealth and honor (22:16–18, 37; 24:11–14)."[35] Balaam was commanded to proclaim only God's words. He acknowledged what God wanted him to do through the events of the donkey narrative particularly.[36] Budd insists that the Yahwist combined the tradition which positively described the sovereignty of Yahweh and the prophetical function of Balaam in the final text.[37]

Olson mentions four characters in the Balaam story: Balak, Balaam, God, and the donkey.[38] Olson evaluates the character of Balaam positively among these four characters. He agrees that it is difficult to assess the character of Balaam decisively through the interpretation of the Bible because the complicated nature of the conglomeration of biblical witnesses has caused the diversity of descriptions of the character of Balaam. However,

---

31. Noth, *Numbers*, 175.

32. Noth, *Numbers*, 175.

33. Budd, *Numbers*, 264. Budd insists that "it would appear therefore that the tendency of the Yahwistic material is to heighten and emphasize elements inherent in the Elohistic base narrative. This supports the view that the Yahwistic material is the accretion rather than the reverse. What the Yahwist here presents is yet more material to give substance to his Transjordanian journey."

34. Budd, *Numbers*, 263.

35. Budd, *Numbers*, 263.

36. Budd, *Numbers*, 264. "The [ass] story also helps to show that there is a basic consistency in Yahweh's attitude. It may appear that v. 20 as compared with v. 12 (both in the Elohistic story) constitutes a change of mind on his part. 'Not so,' says the Yahwist. At the deepest level he is opposed to the whole enterprise, and the permission to go, repeated in v. 35, must be understood in that light. It is fair to add that the ass story was probably highly satirical, with its account of how an ass perceives the angel while the so-called prophet remains blind. Even the beasts are more perceptive than he! In Yahweh's hands, however, Balaam is shown as receiving divine revelation and taking the role of the true penitent (vv 31–34), as well as receiving a true commission (v. 35)."

37. Budd, *Numbers*, 264.

38. Olson, *Numbers*, 140.

Olson insists that Balaam appears "in an essentially positive light" in Num 22–24.[39] He has two reasons for his positive evaluation of Balaam's character. First, even though Balaam was introduced as a negative character in the narrative of the donkey initially, he delivered words of blessing rather than words of cursing.[40] Secondly, as stated in Mic 6:5, Balaam reversed the evil plan of Balak.[41]

Cole's assessment of the character of Balaam is positive overall. He judges Balaam's practice regarding "ritual sacrifice and other divining activities" as being closer to a prophet than a sorcerer.[42] According to him, although Balaam cannot be evaluated as "a faithful believer in Yahweh, God of Israel" because of the reports of other passages in both Testaments and extrabiblical sources, the text of Num 22–24 witnesses that Balaam does do his job, not forcing God to curse Israel but delivering the words of blessing from God toward Israel, sincerely as a diviner or prophet.[43]

Coats insists that the leitmotif of the Balaam story is Balaam delivering the words of God sincerely, and the whole story repeats to report on Balaam's commitment. He contends that the structure of the Balaam story focuses on the character of Balaam as "an ideal figure."[44] For him, Balaam is a positive character for three primary reasons. First, Balaam asked God twice if he should go with Balak's officials or not to confirm God's exact answer. Second, Balaam's commitment was only to God, not to Israel. Third, Balaam rejected the higher honorarium from Balak in the course of his delivering the words of God sincerely.

Negative Evaluations of the Character of Balaam

Wenham points out that the essential chapters in the Balaam story are Num 23–24, and chapter 22 merely shows Balaam's going regardless of

---

39. Olson, *Numbers*, 140.
40. Olson, *Numbers*, 140.
41. Olson, *Numbers*, 140.
42. Cole, *Numbers*, 366. Cole (367) mentions that "Balaam gave no pretense of being a sorcerer who might actually change the will of the God (or even the gods); for he proclaimed, 'I could not do anything great or small to go beyond the command of the Lord my God' (22:18), and again, 'I must speak only what God puts in my mouth' (22:38)."
43. Cole, *Numbers*, 367.
44. Knierim and Coats, *Numbers*, 252.

the credibility of his message.[45] Wenham evaluates Balaam's character negatively for several reasons. First, Balaam's hesitation to go with Balak's officials in the beginning implies that Balaam needed more bribes.[46] Second, the donkey narrative describes Balaam's character comically so that Balaam's character should not be treated seriously or positively by readers. In this donkey narrative, the donkey is portrayed as a true prophet.[47] Finally, "when eventually he does go to curse Israel at Balak's bidding, he pronounces categoric blessings on Israel without equal in the Pentateuch."[48]

Douglas introduces the Balaam story as a play conveying political satire.[49] She points out that Balaam is comically saved by a donkey to prove that the character is more negative than positive in the story. The fact that Balaam accepted Balak's invitation for money is enough for her to judge that Balaam's character is initially evil.

Neutral Evaluations of the Character of Balaam

Gray examines the narrative of the Balaam story in Num 22–24 from the angle of source criticism. He classifies most of the verses in the narrative into J, E, or JE sources.[50] On the issue of Balaam's character, Gray insists that "the writer himself is indifferent to the character of Balaam," even though the fact that Balak's bribe did not corrupt Balaam was a clear subject in J.[51] Balaam is nothing but God's tool carrying out the will of Yahweh.

Milgrom agrees that Num 22:2–21 and Num 22:22–35 are independent units of each other.[52] According to him, the character of Balaam in the donkey narrative (22:22–35) was formed in other passages in the Old and New Testaments and extrabiblical sources. The donkey narrative from these passages and sources portrays Balaam as a funny and wicked character. On the other hand, the narrative of 22:2–21 draws "a picture of Balaam the

---

45. Wenham, *Exploring the Old Testament*, 114.
46. Wenham, *Exploring the Old Testament*, 114.
47. Wenham, *Exploring the Old Testament*, 114–15. Way gave his attention to the role of the talking donkey, and insisted that the donkey played the role of a prophet as a divine agent in the donkey narrative. Way, "Animals in the Prophetic World," 52, 59.
48. Wenham, *Numbers*, 57.
49. Douglas, *In the Wilderness*, 216–34.
50. Gray, *Numbers*, 322–79.
51. Gray, *Numbers*, 318.
52. Milgrom, *Numbers*, 467–69.

saint."[53] Thus, Milgrom determines that Balaam serves a neutral role as a diviner who is God's tool.[54] Milgrom contrasts a diviner "who foretells events but cannot affect them" and a sorcerer "who claims to curse or bless," and categorizes Balaam as a diviner.[55] This view of Milgrom is, strictly speaking, not referring to the character of Balaam, but to his position.

Although Lee is primarily interested in the issue of the connectivity of each paragraph, the structure in the book of Numbers, and the relationship between prose and poetry in the text of Num 22–24, he does state his position on the character of Balaam.[56] He insists that the story of Balaam and the donkey stands not to report on the positive or negative evaluation of Balaam's character but to deliver the message that Balak's plan was initially wrong. Therefore, the question of whether Balaam's character is positive or negative is secondary and not significant in the text itself.

Mann reads the Balaam story as a power game between Yahweh, who is the God of Israel, and Balaam, who is a pagan diviner. He is interested in the character of Balaam, who has an international reputation, and the tension between Yahweh and Balaam around the issue of blessing and cursing the people of Israel, even though Balaam turned to bless Israel later.[57]

Notably, in his dissertation, Moore examines the role of Balaam by using a comparative phenomenological view of both the Old Testament and the Deir ʿAllā texts.[58] His interest in the role of Balaam seems to be developed from the study of diviners/seers/exorcists in the settings of selected ancient Near Eastern magico-religious specialists, Balaam Bar Beor at Deir ʿAllā and Balaam Ben Beor in the Bible. His determination that the role of Balaam as diviner/seer and exorcist as depicted in the biblical texts and the Deir ʿAllā texts overlaps leads to the conclusion that the character of Balaam is "not a simple figure, but a complex one enacting a plurality of roles."[59] Although his study is not limited to Num 22–24, his comparative study on Balaam's role with the materials of ancient Anatolia, Mesopotamia, and Syria-Palestine sheds light on Balaam's actions and functions.

---

53. Milgrom, *Numbers*, 469.
54. Milgrom, *Numbers*, 471–73.
55. Milgrom, *Numbers*, 471.
56. Lee, *Punishment and Forgiveness*, 168–72.
57. Mann, *The Book of the Torah*, 169–74.
58. Moore, *The Balaam Traditions*, 66–109.
59. Moore, *The Balaam Traditions*, 109.

Ashley insists that although many scholars have interpreted the character of Balaam within Num 22–24 according to their own preconceived notions, the text of the Balaam story in Num 22–24 is not genuinely interested in the issue of Balaam's character.[60] According to him, the character of Balaam in the story of Num 22–24 is incidental. He rightly insists that "it must be stressed that, whatever Balaam finally did, and whatever later tradition judged him to be, on the basis of the current text only a neutral judgment can be made."[61] Further, he insists that Balaam is nothing but a tool to accomplish God's purpose.

As stated above, scholars are interested in the character of Balaam and have tried to justify their positions of positive, negative, and neutral evaluations. However, their conclusions vary according to their methodologies. Why is there no consensus on the issue of the character of Balaam among scholars? The answer to this question and the reason that I stand on the side of a neutral evaluation of Balaam's character is that, first, the original text of the Balaam story in Num 22–24 seems to be silent on Balaam's character, not giving obvious indications regarding his wrongdoings; and, second, agreeing with Ashley's viewpoint, the text seems not to be interested in the character of Balaam because his role is merely that of a tool, a messenger of God.

Studies on the Features of the Narrative and the Oracles in the Balaam Story

Besides a few studies such as semantic analysis of the oracles of Balaam, form-critical and source-critical studies have also been carried out on the text.[62] Van Seters examines the story of Balaam on the basis of the documentary hypothesis, and continues his discussion on the issues of "the prose and the poetic oracles within the broader comparative context and

---

60. Ashley, *The Book of Numbers*, 435.
61. Ashley, *The Book of Numbers*, 435.
62. Notarius, "Poetic Discourse," 55. Notarius introduces "a semantic analysis of the verbal tenses to the biblical poetic discourse" with the case study of the oracles of Balaam and insists that "(1) the verbal forms in the poetic text are analyzed according to the universal semantic and pragmatic parameters; (2) the distinctive linear character of the poetic text (the parallelism) has no decisive influence on the semantic value of the verbal categories; (3) the functioning of verbal tenses in the biblical poetic text is not necessarily similar to their functioning in prosaic conversation."

Who Is the True Seer Driven by God?

the tradition history of the Balaam tradition generally."[63] Knierim and Coats argue that the Balaam story serves "the Yahwistic source as a key for the divine appointment of kingship for Israel/Jacob."[64] For them, the blessing from Yahweh toward Israel is a Yahwistic expression for the victory and intimacy that Yahweh possesses for his people Israel.

However, source criticism has the disadvantage of not being able to answer the question of structural unity created by the literary motives and factors that lead to this story. It is more helpful to observe the employed literary expressions in the text to understand the various aspects of the Balaam story described in Num 22–24 than study the history of the development of the materials.[65]

Levine suspects that the Balaam story is a separate unit, but the narrative of the donkey is interpolated into the story.[66] He concludes that the existence of the narrative of the donkey in the story is the result of the later inserted negative tradition of Balaam.[67] He insists that "the author of this picaresque tale" (22:22–35) juxtaposed the narrative of the donkey with the primary Balaam tradition and caused "pejorative characterization of Balaam" in the whole Balaam story.[68] According to him, the text of Num 22–24 is an independent unit regardless of the documentary sources of J and E. However, it is difficult to assert that the same author could have produced the narratives of 22:2–21 and 22:22–35.

Milgrom insists that the independent Balaam story later included the narrative of the donkey, which contains negative reflections of the character of Balaam primarily formed by the reports on Balaam from other texts in the Old and New Testaments as well as extrabiblical traditions.[69] He

---

63. Van Seters, *The Life of Moses*, 405.

64. Knierim and Coats, *Numbers*, 246–62.

65. Cf. Tosato, "The Literary Structure," 98. Tosato introduces the literary structure of the poems of Balaam: "the first two poems of Balaam (Num 23:7–10 and 23:18–24), commonly ascribed to E, are composed according to the stylistic principle of concentric symmetry, the strophes being organized in a scheme A-B-A' (first poem) and A-B-C-B'-A' (second poem)."

66. Levine, *Numbers 21–36*, 137–39. Even for the scholars who treat the Balaam story as an independent unit, it is difficult to solve the issues such as the birth of the Balaam story as a unified one and the authorship of the whole story. Thus, the presupposition of the donkey narrative's interpolation could be a solution for the issues.

67. Levine, *Numbers 21–36*, 154.

68. Levine, *Numbers 21–36*, 155.

69. Milgrom, *Numbers*, 468–69.

suggests various reasons for the inconsistency of the donkey episode with the previous narrative: (1) "Balak and the Moabites have disappeared from the scene"; (2) "heretofore, it was Balak who pitted himself against God, now it is Balaam"; (3) "Balaam, hitherto the compliant servant of God, now openly defies him by consenting to curse Israel without his permission."[70] According to him, the purpose of the donkey narrative is "doubtless the humiliation of Balaam, evidenced by the strain of irony that runs through the entire pericope" and "downgrading Balaam's reputation by demonstrating that this heathen seer, who was intent on cursing Israel without God's consent, is in reality a fool, a caricature of a seer, one outwitted even by his dumb beast."[71]

Milgrom also suggests the unity of the prose and poetry in chapters 22–24 in the sense that "the poetry was composed for the sake of the prose, and the poetic oracles would make no sense without the narrative."[72] According to him, "the poetic oracles and the narrative were originally independent of each other, discrete epics on the same theme, which were fused at a later date by a single editorial hand."[73] Thus, he seems to assert that three distinct units, Num 22:2–21 (the primary narrative), 22:22–35 (the donkey narrative), and the poetic oracle sections, were combined by an editor to form unity in the Balaam story in Num 22–24.

However, some presuppositions are needed to solidify the arguments of Levine and Milgrom above. Several questions reveal the presuppositions. First, does the donkey narrative really convey the negative tradition of Balaam, including the message of Balaam's humiliation? Second, does Balaam change his attitude from a good servant of God to an evil sorcerer against God? Third, does Balaam go to Balak to curse Israel without the permission of God? Last, is the assumption that the Balaam story in Num 22–24 has unity by the work of an editor credible? It is necessary to undertake an exegetical analysis of the Balaam story in Num 22–24 to examine the legitimacy of the arguments.

Coats insists that the donkey narrative in the Balaam story is a distinct story derived from a different tradition on Balaam, and "the problem [of the issue of the donkey narrative's interpolation] is a traditio-historical one,

---

70. Milgrom, *Numbers*, 468.
71. Milgrom, *Numbers*, 469.
72. Milgrom, *Numbers*, 467.
73. Milgrom, *Numbers*, 468.

not a source-critical one."[74] He also mentions the issue of the relation of the use of various divine names to the functional coherence of the story. For him, the occurrences of various divine names are not because of varying sources, but because of "the patterns of the leitmotif." He insists that the hand of the Yahwist formed the Balaam story, and it is "functionally coherent."[75] However, it is worth noting that Coats considers the Balaam story as belonging to the Yahwist despite not treating the Balaam text from a source-critical viewpoint. He does not mention issues of the thematic or theological coherence of the Balaam story. Nevertheless, he rightly notices that the structure of the donkey narrative of Num 22:22–35 "emphasized the act of seeing."[76]

Ashley acknowledges the difficulty of the donkey narrative's harmony within the Balaam story. According to him, it seems reasonable to conclude that the donkey narrative that already existed as an independent unit was interpolated into the Balaam story later, even though it is difficult to prove when and how the interpolation happened, and it is accepted that the narrative's location in the literary context of the story is easily discerned.[77]

Most scholars who cannot support the unity of the Balaam story have difficulty solving the problem of the donkey narrative's interpolation. On the one hand, a primary reason to insist that the donkey narrative is not in accord within the Balaam story and was interpolated into the story is that readers focus on the character of Balaam in the narrative. On the other hand, one possible solution for the issue of the donkey narrative's interpolation is to abandon a view that focuses on the character of Balaam in the narrative to find, instead, the central message of the narrative as a whole. By considering other thematic or topical elements besides Balaam's character in order to illuminate the central message of the Balaam story, we will be able to solidify the unity of the donkey narrative with the overarching Balaam story.

---

74. Knierim and Coats, *Numbers*, 260.
75. Knierim and Coats, *Numbers*, 260.
76. Knierim and Coats, *Numbers*, 261.
77. Ashley, *The Book of Numbers*, 435, 454.

Studies on the Relationship between the Prose and Poetic Sections of the Balaam Story

Van Seters insists that the poetic sections are older than the prose parts, and they are the core elements to form the Balaam tradition. According to him, "the relationship between the poetic oracles and the prose narrative has likewise been a matter of long discussion. It is the assumption of many of the studies of the Balaam pericope that the poetic oracles are older, originally independent, pieces and therefore the oldest part of the tradition."[78]

Levine treats the Balaam story not from the perspective of the documentary sources of J and E, even though he mentions J and E sources, but from an interest in the composition and relationship of the narrative and poetic sections.[79] According to Levine, the poems in the Balaam story should be dated earlier than the narratives because they utilize different divine names.[80] The narratives further developed the themes of the poems, and offer differing perspectives. Thus, he concludes that the author of the narratives in the Balaam story is different from the poem's author.

Milgrom, on the basis of Rabbinic tradition, believes that "the Balaam story was composed independently and later inserted into the Pentateuchal corpus."[81] He examines the separation of the story, the interpolation of the donkey narrative, the character of Balaam, the profession of Balaam, and the Balaam inscription. On the issue of the relationship between the prose and the poetry in the Balaam story, Milgrom agrees that the prosaic parts and the poetic sections might be "originally independent of each other."[82] However, he insists on the redactional possibility for the organic unity between the narrative and the poetry in the Balaam story. According to him, a skillful editor at a later date compiled the existing narrative (except for the donkey narrative) and the poetry in a well-formed thematic flow. While this solution makes questions of chronology and authorship of the individual poetry and prose sections partially moot, it does not solve the problem of the donkey narrative's interpolation within the whole Balaam story as a whole.

---

78. Van Seters, *The Life of Moses*, 407.

79. Levine, *Numbers 21–36*, 207–08.

80. Levine, *Numbers 21–36*, 209, 234.

81. Milgrom, *Numbers*, 185.

82. Milgrom, *Numbers*, 467–68.

Conclusion

As stated above, scholars have examined the text of Num 22–24, namely the Balaam story, from various perspectives, showing interest in the sources of the documents beyond the text and the texts from Deir 'Allā inscription, and have drawn conclusions based on evaluations of depictions of Balaam's character, the features of the narratives and the oracles, and the relationship between the prose section and the poetic collection. These studies contribute to understanding the given text in light of literary/linguistic analyses of prominent features of the text as well as the background and processes of the formation of the text.

This survey demonstrates that these scholars' conclusions are based almost entirely on the methodology they use, by which I mean that none of them were surprised at what they found when they analyzed the text with the tools they like to use, and the results typically reduce the text to fragments. The scholars' works help to illuminate certain aspects of the narrative, but none of them offer a convincing solution to all the problems I point out. More importantly, it shows the possibility for, and the importance of, further discussion about additional steps to be taken to determine the intention and message of the Balaam text.

I concur with Ashely that focusing on the literary and theological aspects of the text of the Balaam story is a helpful starting point and leads to the conclusion that Balaam is a mere tool of God to deliver his message and accomplish his purpose.[83] This viewpoint also helps us to account for the unity of the text of Num 22–24, which has a central theme and message.

In the next chapter, I will introduce my methodology, which will allow for discovering the intention and the message of the Balaam story in Num 22–24 as well as suggesting a possible way to recognize the unity of the text. I will also apply this methodology to the given text to demonstrate its effectiveness.

---

83. Ashley, *The Book of Numbers*, 435.

Chapter 2

Methodology for the Study and Its Application to the Analysis of the Balaam Text of Num 22–24

Introduction

IN CHAPTER 1, I identified and attempted to introduce the scholarly discussions regarding some issues of the Balaam story in Num 22–24. The selected issues are: 1) whether the Balaam story[1] tells about the character of Balaam, 2) the relationship between Num 22:2–20 and Num 22:21–35, and 3) whether unity exists between the prose section and the poetic collection.

In this chapter, I will identify and attempt to answer the raised questions. To answer the questions, it is necessary to introduce my method for the study and its application to the analysis of the Balaam text of Num 22–24. Especially, this study, which deals with a mixed collection of prose and poetic texts, aspires to be an example of a holistic approach to the prose

1. Heimerdinger, *Topic, Focus and Foreground*, 42–43. Heimerdinger introduces the concepts of "story" and "narrative," which are "often used interchangeably . . . Narrative refers to a general group of narrated genres. It designates an inclusive category comprising various specific forms such as story or account of events. When a narrative is concerned with simply reporting a temporal sequence of events, we are dealing with an 'account of events' . . . As for the story, it is intrinsically more complicated in its shape than as account of events . . . Many definitions of story, however, emphasize the particular role of plot. By plot is meant a particular pattern which presents a flow of action from one state of balance (beginning) to another state of balance (resolution) through an intervening process of disequilibrium or imbalance (middle). A plot progresses from an activating starting point through the stage of complication to a peak or point of climax. From there, the plotline descends to a resolved ending, or denouement, and a closure."

and the poetry, in contrast to the phenomena whereby most scholars research texts on the one side or the other on the spectrum. Interestingly, even on the study of the Balaam story in Num 22–24, it is difficult to find scholars who deal with the text as a well-woven composite of prose as well as poetry.[2] However, I will show how the intention and message of a mixed text like this can be grasped as a story. In addition, I shall consider the role of Balaam and the relationship between the two prose-narratives in the Balaam story. Ultimately, these examinations will be helpful to disclose the purpose of the Balaam story in Num 22–24.

Methodology

Introduction

My methodology is a mixture of a text linguistic and literary analysis.[3] A literary analysis is useful since the two main concerns of this study are the

---

2. Tosato, "The Literary Structure," 98–106; Notarius, "Poetic Discourse," 55–86; Albright, "The Oracles of Balaam," 207–33; Begg, "Balaam's Talking Ass," 207–28; Way, "Animals in the Prophetic World," 47–62; Jones, "Balaam, Pagan Prophet of God," 123–67.

3. Provan et al., *A Biblical History of Israel*, 80–81. They describe the advantages and disadvantages of literary readings and historical studies: "As Gale Yee notes, literary (i.e., 'text-centered') approaches can indeed give rise to problems: 'severing the text from its author and history could result in an ahistorical inquiry that regards the text primarily as an aesthetic object unto itself rather than a social practice intimately bound to a particular history' . . . Most biblical texts were not composed as 'pure' literature (i.e., art for art's sake), but as 'applied' literature ('history, liturgy, laws, preaching, and the like'). They are not 'autotelic'—to use T. S. Eliot's coinage for a literary work that has 'no end or purpose beyond its own existence.' On the contrary, they often instruct, recount, exhort, or some combination of these and more. What this means is that literature and history cannot be regarded as unrelated, or mutually exclusive, categories . . . It becomes obvious, then, that literary understanding is a necessary condition of historical understanding, and both literary and historical understanding are necessary conditions of competent biblical interpretation. As Robert Alter aptly puts it, 'In all biblical narrative and in a good deal of biblical poetry as well, the domain in which literary invention and religious imagination are joined is history, for all these narratives, with the exception of Job and possibly Jonah, purport to be true accounts of things that have occurred in historical time.' Simply put, much of the Bible makes historical truth claims, and these claims will never be rightly understood unless the literary mode of their representation is itself understood. Again, Alter is helpful: 'For a reader to attend to these elements of literary art is not merely an exercise in "appreciation" but a discipline of understanding: the literary vehicle is so much the necessary medium through which the Hebrew writers realized their meanings that we will grasp the meanings at best imperfectly if we ignore their

context and message of the text.⁴ A text linguistic analysis is helpful in order to discern the text's intensions through studying the linguistic expressions used in the Balaam story in Num 22–24.⁵ Therefore, the presupposition of the text linguistic and literary methodology in this study is that a text is a field of communication in which an implied author indicates the message

---

fine articulations as literature' . . . Our aim in this section has been simply to establish that a happy marriage between literary and historical concerns is possible, desirable, and necessary. The ahistorical path is a dead end. Where biblical texts make historical truth claims, ahistorical readings are perforce misreadings—which remains the case, whatever one's opinions may be regarding the truth value of those claims."

4. Robert Alter, *The Art of Biblical Narrative*, 13. Alter describes literary analysis as "the manifold varieties of minutely discriminating attention to the artful use of language, to the shifting play of ideas, conventions, tone, sound, imagery, syntax, narrative viewpoint, compositional units, and much else; the kind of disciplined attention, in other words, that through a whole spectrum of critical approaches has illuminated, for example, the poetry of Dante, the plays of Shakespeare, the novels of Tolstoy." Provan et al., *A Biblical History of Israel*, 88, 90–93, comment on the reading of narrative historiography: "In the present chapter, we have sought to talk seriously about biblical historiographical narrative as both art and history, not in terms of some fifty-fifty, fiction-fact mixture but in terms of true history artfully presented . . . The key point is that biblical account must be appreciated first as narratives before they can be used as historical sources—just as they cannot be dismissed as historical sources simply because of their narrative form. Indeed, it is not just biblical narratives but ancient Near Eastern texts in general that show literary patterns and shaping . . . It is worth noting that this listing of questions historians should ask is quite similar to listings of questions that literary readers of the Bible should ask. In his recent book on the Bible's narrative art, Jan Fokkelman presents the following list of ten questions designed to facilitate careful and competent reading of biblical narratives: 1. Hero 2. Quest 3. The helpers and the antagonists 4. The narrator 5. Chronology 6. Narrated time 7. Plot 8. Dialogue 9. Word choice, style or structure 10. Unit regarding theme."

5. De Beaugrande and Dressler, *Introduction to Text Linguistics*, 14. I do not use the term "text linguistics" in the sense of a specific fixed theory. Text linguistics is a field of linguistics that studies features and the use of a text. Text linguistics is not a fixed or unified theoretical system. Various sub-methodologies have been introduced under the term of "text linguistics." According to Beaugrande and Dressler, "text linguistics cannot in fact be a designation for a single theory or method. Instead, it designates any work in language science devoted to the text as the primary object of inquiry." Therefore, I use the term in an inclusive and general form. In my dissertation, I will define the tools and terms that I employ as I make use of them throughout the study.

Talstra's comments on "textlinguistics" are apt in relation to defining its meaning and scope: "Textlinguistics, however, seeks to reclaim part of the text-level analysis for the study of the linguistic system, rather than leave it the exclusive purview of scholars dealing with views on ancient authors' freedom of literary design . . . Textlinguistics compares linguistic phenomena not only to a pattern or a paradigm of constructions, but also to a more abstract functional matrix, such as the function of clause connections." Talstra, "Text Linguistics: Biblical Hebrew," 755–60.

not by a meaningless arrangement of sentences, but by a whole integrated unit, and that readers can find the message and the intention of the text by examining the text linguistically and literarily.[6]

In this study I will primarily utilize the text-linguistic methodology of Jean-Marc Heimerdinger in *Topic, Focus and Foreground in Ancient Hebrew Narratives*.[7] Although I do not accept or apply the entirety of Heimerdinger's theory to the text of the Balaam story in Num 22–24, I will use certain points of his work to illuminate this study of the text of the Balaam story. I will also utilize other text-linguistic approaches, introducing and defining terms when necessary.

There are two sections of prose and poetry in the text of Num 22–24. As noted already, and contrary to other scholars, my methodology does not divide the text based on literary genres of prose and poetry because I believe that the text consists of a story that is internally consistent in its intention and message. At this point, my methodology departs from Heimerdinger's theory; although Heimerdinger himself never insisted his theory should be applied to the prose genre exclusively, he effectively only examines narratives. In this section, I will not be introducing or discussing Heimerdinger's theory in detail. Instead, I will present my methodology for this study.

Heimerdinger discusses ideas of "topic" and "focus" in his work. He explicitly defines "topic" as "the starting point of an utterance . . . a term to describe what a text is all about; its subject matter."[8] The subject, as topic, tends to persist throughout the discourse. The main subject or participant of the discourse tends to have the role of agent. "Focus" is "the most important piece of new information mentioned by the speaker . . . the referent is in focus because it stands in a pragmatic relation to the proposition in such a way that its addition to the proposition produces an utterance which is a piece of new information."[9] Whereas Heimerdinger's discussion of topic and focus centers on nouns, nominal phrases, subjects, referents or participants, my discussion will center on verbs.[10] Most of the suggestions that

---

6. Jeanrond, *Theological Hermeneutics*, 84. "A text is more than the sum of its words or sentences. A text is a meaningful whole, a structured whole."

7. Heimerdinger, *Topic, Focus and Foreground*, 101–260.

8. Heimerdinger, *Topic, Focus and Foreground*, 101–02.

9. Heimerdinger, *Topic, Focus and Foreground*, 163–64.

10. Many biblical Hebrew scholars are interested in the discussion regarding topic and focus; cf. Givón, Rosenbaum, Buth, Holmstedt, Van der Merwe, Naudé, Kroeze, Heimerdinger, Talstra, Shimasaki. For more detailed introductions and discussions on the issue of topic and focus, refer to Floor, "From Information Structure," 19–188.

comprise my methodology below thus result from this major difference from Heimerdinger's viewpoints and mine.

The Exegetical Viewpoint

The most fundamental basis of the methodology in this study is to interpret the text of Num 22–24 with an exegetical interest in what the text tells and intends. That is, this methodology is employed to disclose the message of the text, not to build another theory in the text linguistics field. Therefore, I will introduce the works of Heimerdinger, only borrowing his insights into the exegetical sense of the text but not discussing his text-linguistic theory itself.

Heimerdinger employs an exegetical viewpoint that focuses on the intention of biblical texts in his interpretational studies.[11] In other words, although he interacts with other text-linguistic scholars' theories, his arguments deal more with the exegetical interpretation of biblical texts.

However, Heimerdinger's approach does have a weakness. Though he explicitly engages the interrelationship between topic, focus, and foreground, he does not show how the foreground especially reveals the intention and the message of the text. As Floor points out, the exegetical interests of Heimerdinger in the chapter on foreground are not dependent on his previous chapters regarding topic and focus.[12] In addition, it is difficult to

---

11. Heimerdinger, *Topic, Focus and Foreground*, 221–60. Heimerdinger introduces related passages from the Old Testament in each example of his explanations in the book. He also writes one chapter on the subject of foreground, which deals with the intention and the message of the text.

12. Floor, "From Information Structure," 233–34. Floor finds "it unfortunate in Heimerdinger's approach to foregrounding (and by implication, theme analysis) that he notices all the correct starting points without following through to integrate information structure with an integrated theory of foregrounding. He develops an elaborate description of information structure in Biblical Hebrew (chapters 4 and 5), but doesn't look there in depth for answers to foregrounding." He also quotes Heimerdinger to show how he considers topic important: "Topical importance is the central dimension of topicality, and the title provides a good indication as to which entities are the main topical ones in the story" (Heimerdinger, *Topic, Focus and Foreground*, 108). "But computation will show it in a more precise way. Levels of topical importance can be determined by examining semantic roles. Actor/agent role more dominant, and when it coincides with an important undergoer, gains even more prominence" (Heimerdinger, *Topic, Focus and Foreground*, 116–7). "A topic is salient in terms of attention, the topic who is in control" (Heimerdinger, *Topic, Focus and Foreground*, 126). "One may conclude that the grammatical encoding of topical entities is a significant indicator of topical importance in Old

find the correlation between topic and focus in his theory and suggestions.[13] On the contrary, my exegetical interest in the Balaam text of Num 22–24 is consistently dependent on the topical verb, which will be the beginning point of my discussions in this study, along with other topically-related verbs, in order to show the topicality of the whole text in the sense of delivering the intention and the message of the text.

Nonetheless, the heading theory of Heimerdinger is important for the methodology of this study. The approach is not only the starting point of his theory but also suggests the exegetical framework of a narrative reading of the OT. The exegetical viewpoint of Heimerdinger through the heading theory is the common ground of this methodology. I will introduce the heading theory and the difference between Heimerdinger's approach and mine in more detail in what follows.

Appraisal of the Traditional Theory of the Role of *Vayyiqtol*

One of Heimerdinger's outstanding contributions is suggesting the inappropriateness of the functional explanation that centers on the verbal form of *vayyiqtol* for the main storyline, and the verbal form of *we-X-qatal* for the secondary background.[14] For him, it is not reasonable that the specific form of a verb or the combination of a verb and other elements (such as a conjunction or a subject) is crucial to demonstrate the main plotline of a narrative and distinguish the foreground and background of a story. Heimerdinger has successfully taken the discussion of such things as foregrounding beyond the level of analyzing verbal forms in individual sentences. Any kind of obvious occurrence of *we-X-qatal* is not found in the first sentence of a new (changed) scene or an explanation of the background in the Balaam story. The dichotomous division might be persuasive for shorter narratives, but it is difficult to expect the same in longer stories in the OT. That is, it is too simple to explain the mechanism of the Hebrew narrative's main plotline and the secondary background with only the form of a verb.

Hebrew narrative" (Heimerdinger, *Topic, Focus and Foreground*, 116).

13. Heimerdinger provides the passage of Gen 22 as the case study of topic in chapter 3, which discusses topicality and topical entities, but he doesn't deal with focus in the same passage to show how topic and focus work interrelatedly.

14. Heimerdinger, *Topic, Focus and Foreground*, 79.

Analysis of the Balaam Text of Num 22–24

On the Terms of Topic and Topicality

Heimerdinger introduces the topicality and topical entity as below.

> The heading announces the topic of the story: God tested Abraham. The discourse topic comprises one central action (to test) with two topical entities Abraham and God, which are topical participants. Through the heading these two participants are assigned the highest degree of topical importance and it is expected that such a feature should be reflected at clause level."[15]

Heimerdinger also suggests how to determine the topical importance of entities as below:

> Topical importance has a mainly cataphoric character: topical entities which are important persist in the developing discourse and so occur with greater frequency than less important ones ... Tomlin proposes a calculation method which he calls "computing of cumulative referential density" ...
>
> These figures would seem to indicate that topical importance is not only simply connected to the persistence or the recurrence of an entity in the discourse, but is also significantly correlated to the S function of the entity ... A main topical entity may not always be realized as S, but topical importance would seem to coincide with S.[16]
>
> One may conclude that the grammatical encoding of topical entities is a significant indicator of topical importance in Old Hebrew narrative ... In the ice-hockey game report, Tomlin mentions

---

15. Heimerdinger, *Topic, Focus and Foreground*, 106. The concept of "discourse topic" for Heimerdinger is equivalent to that of "thematic information" for Tomlin: information held in common by speaker and hearer that is connected to the goal of the discourse. Heimerdinger insists that the participants (characters) have the highest degree of topical importance, but does not explain why only nouns (characters) have this status to the exclusion of verbs. In addition, his presupposition seems to exclude the topicality of a verb that is a "central action" from his argument regarding the topicality of the whole text. His presupposition of and interest in the concepts of topicality and topical hierarchy also seem to be limited to nouns and nominal phrases. I disagree with this approach, and contend that it could be accepted only if a text intentionally introduces the main character (a topical entity) and the central action together in the heading of a given text, such as in Gen 22, which is Heimerdinger's example. However, this approach is not persuasive when a text introduces a secondary character who doesn't have the highest degree of the topical entity in the heading, such as in Num 22–24. I will treat this more in detail later in this section.

16. Heimerdinger, *Topic, Focus and Foreground*, 115.

a player in control of the puck as an example of a referent higher in topicality than a reference to the puck which has become loose.[17]

Heimerdinger added the introduction of Tomlin's model for topicality. "Such statistical analysis is based on the fact that referents which are more important occur more often than less important referents."[18] Heimerdinger, agreeing with Tomlin, seems to suggest that characters have a higher topicality than verbs in a given text. However, the problem is that Heimerdinger cannot explain how the central "action" (to test), which is the term Heimerdinger employs, is thematically woven through an entire narrative. I suggest, then, that one cannot determine topicality through an analysis of characters themselves, and that only when characters are related and connected with topical verbs and the related sub-topical verbs do the characters have topicality. That is, the topicality of characters is dependent on topical verbs.

Two viewpoints of Heimerdinger from his chapter on topicality and topical entities should be considered. First, Heimerdinger distinguishes "topic" from "topicality," and treats the notion of "topic" at the level of clause.[19] Second, although Heimerdinger differentiates the concepts of

17. Heimerdinger, *Topic, Focus and Foreground*, 116.

18. Heimerdinger, *Topic, Focus and Foreground*, 104.

19. Dooley, "Explorations in Discourse Topicality," 79. Dooley subdivides "topic" into "discourse topic" and "sentence topic": "In some sense, discourse topics are what a particular discourse unit is about, just as sentence topics are what a sentence (or utterance) is about." See also Brown and Yule, *Discourse Analysis*, 70–71: "A distinction can be made between the topic and the comment in a sentence. In that 'the speaker announces a topic and then says something about it . . . Topics are usually also subjects and comments are predicates . . . A sentential topic may coincide with the grammatical subject. The term 'topic', then, as found in descriptions of sentence structure, is essentially a term which identifies a particular sentential constituent. It has also been used by Givón in his argument that, in the development of a language, sentential subjects are derived from 'grammaticalised topics'. However, we are not, for the moment, concerned with the structure of linguistic units comparable to the simple sentence. Nor are we considering 'topic' as a grammatical constituent of any kind. We are primarily interested in the general pretheoretical notion of 'topic' as 'what is being talked about' in a conversation. This type of 'topic' is unlikely to be identifiable as one part of a sentence . . . In an attempt to distinguish their notion of topic from the grammarians' sentential topic, Keenan and Schieffelin (1976) used the term 'discourse topic.' What Keenan and Schieffelin emphasize is that 'discourse topic is not a simple NP, but a proposition' . . . in describing the discourse topic as the 'question of immediate concern.' The implication in their study is that there must be, for any fragment of conversational discourse, a single proposition which represents the discourse topic of the whole of the fragment. Such a view is certainly too simplistic, as we hope to show by considering some experimental work in which 'the topic' was treated

topic and topicality, he limits the discussion regarding topic and topicality to nominal elements or participants such as subjects, and seems to equivocate the meaning of topic, subject, and referent so that the concepts of topic and topicality are interchangeable. These two viewpoints of Heimerdinger reveal the inconsistency between the two:

> Any utterance has a subject or topic and something is said about this topic, which is the comment. So the topic constitutes the starting point of an utterance ... There seems to be a general consensus among linguists that clause topic is "what the clause is going to be about." This is the definition of clause topic which will be adopted in this chapter. Topic is the entity that the proposition communicated in the clause is about. As such the topic of a clause is the referential material which provides a plug-in point for the comment, the comment having the specific function of "point-making."
>
> Topicality is viewed not as a clause-dependent property only but as a discourse-dependent one as well: what makes a participant topical is not the fact that it is grammatically coded as topical in a sentence, but rather that it is the topic of the discourse or a stretch of discourse. The discourse-based approach will provide the starting point for the study which follows, a topic (what a sentence is about) being viewed as dependent upon the context of communication.
>
> Topicality is best described cognitively as the centering of attention of speaker and hearer on discourse entities which are the main concern of the story.[20]

According to Heimerdinger, ideas of topic and topicality have not been explored with any level of detailed research.[21] The definitions and relationship of topic and topicality have remained muddled to linguistic or text-linguistic scholars.[22]

---

as the equivalent of a title."

20. Heimerdinger, *Topic, Focus and Foreground*, 101–03, 125.

21. Heimerdinger, *Topic, Focus and Foreground*, 101.

22. Givón, *Topic Continuity in Discourse*, cover endorsement: "The functional notion of 'topic' or 'topicality' has suffered, traditionally, from two distinct drawbacks. First, it has remained largely ill defined or intuitively defined. And second, quite often its definition boiled down to structure-dependent circularity. This volume represents a major departure from past practices, without rejecting both their intuitive appeal and the many good results yielded by them. First, 'topic' and 'topicality' are re-analyzed as a scalar property, rather than as an either/or discrete prime. Second, the graded property of 'topicality' is firmly connected with sensible cognitive notions culled from gestalt psychology, such as 'predictability' or 'continuity'. Third, we develop and utilize precise measures and

Since the primary concern of this study is not to discuss the relationship between topic and topicality on a theoretical linguistic or text-linguistic level, but to examine what the story in the text of Num 22–24 is about and what it intends to convey, when I use the term "topical" in conjunction with verb(s), I will not focus on the linguistic concepts of topic and topicality or participate in the aforementioned linguistic and text-linguistic discussions. Instead, I will use the term "topical" with regard to the verb(s) used by the implied author of the text to introduce, develop and intensify the message and the intention of the text. I believe that the topicality of the Balaam story in Num 22–24, what the text is "about," can be grasped through investigating the verb(s) in the first sentence of the heading in the text. Therefore, it is essential to define the topical verb(s) as the key verb(s) conveying the primary message and intention of a given text.

The Importance of Verb

In this section, I will discuss the role of verbs in a paragraph or a whole text rather than merely in a sentence.[23] Scholars have debated issues regarding the role and function of the verbal form and word order in both narratival and poetic genres, but have not reached a consensus.[24] On the other hand,

---

quantified methods by which the property of 'topicality' of clausal arguments can be studied in connected discourse, and thus be properly hinged in its rightful context, that of topic identification, maintenance, and recoverability in discourse. Fourth, we show that many grammatical phenomena which used to be studied by linguists in isolation all partake in one functional domain of grammar, that of topic identification. Finally, we demonstrate the validity of this new approach to the study of 'topic' and 'topicality' by applying the same text-based quantifying method to a number of typologically-diverse languages in studying actual texts."

23. Robar, *The Verb and the Paragraph in Biblical Hebrew*, 61. "The discussions over the biblical Hebrew verbs have often centered on whether their function is primarily at the clause level (for tense, aspect, and modality) or equally at a higher level, a discourse level. Discussions on the higher discourse level of the paragraph have been anything but uniform. Some refer strictly to morphosyntactic criteria (e.g., morphological form and word order), others to speaker orientation (e.g., narrative vs. direct speech) and others to discourse pragmatics (e.g., foreground vs. background)."

24. Kamp, *Inner Worlds*, 38, 40; "In more recent grammatical descriptions of biblical Hebrew, verbs are studied with regard to their position in the sentence and to their communicative function in relation to the reader. Weinrich's theory of language is generally taken as the basis for this, in which the tense and aspectual value of the verb no longer occupies a central position in the grammatical and syntactic description of sentences and sentence-parts . . . In linguistic research the syntactic framework of the text as a whole

Analysis of the Balaam Text of Num 22–24

I suggest to invoke the lack of consensus as an invitation to explore other options such as the one I choose.

Brueggemann denotes the importance of verbs in the narratives of the OT:

> At the core of Israel's theological grammar are sentences governed by strong verbs of transformation. Such sentences are so familiar to us that we may fail to notice the oddity of their grammar and therefore neglect such a theological beginning point. This focus on sentences signifies that Israel is characteristically concerned with the action of God—the concrete, specific action of God—and not God's character, nature, being, or attributes, except as those are evidenced in concrete actions. This focus on verbs, moreover, commits us in profound ways to a *narrative* portrayal of Yahweh, in which Yahweh is the one who is said to have done these deeds. In what follows, I will consider, as a beginning point, the verbs that stand characteristically at the center of Israel's narrative testimony to Yahweh's action.[25]

He introduces specific verbs that show the actions of Yahweh in the Hebrew narratives of the OT: the God who creates (יצר, דבר, קנה, עשׂה, ברה), the God who promises (דבר, שׁבע), the God who delivers (גאל, עלה, ישׁע, פדה, יצא), the God who commands (צוה), and the God who guides (נחה, נהל), feeds (אכל), and tests (נסה).[26]

Though Brueggemann examines the role and importance of verbs only in the context of the actions of Yahweh, I propose that verbs in any narrative have the most crucial role of relating the narratives' themes and intentions. Of course, not every verb in a text can be treated as one involved in the theme-making process. Thus, regarding the relationship between verbs and the theme of a text, it is most helpful to determine the topical verb(s) of the text. I will discuss this further in a following section.

In conclusion, I will suggest that verbs and verbs + characters are critical when attempting to determine the primary plotline and message of a

---

is important, and this is why Weinrich speaks of text linguistics. This means that the morphological features of a morpheme are determined by the syntactic functions that it fulfils in the text as a whole. The form of a verb thus no longer determines the function, but the communicative function in the text determines the specific form." Kamp suggests a different view on the relation of the form of a verb and its function from the traditional view, in which the form of a verb determines the function.

25. Brueggemann, *Theology of the Old Testament*, 145.
26. Brueggemann, *Theology of the Old Testament*, 145–212.

narrative. As I will demonstrate, the verb is the primary element in a narrative, both in sentences and groups of paragraphs, that carries the meaning throughout a particular story.

The Topical Verb(s)

The Heading of Topic Framework in a Text

Heimerdinger, borrowing Tomlin's theory, introduces how to grasp the topicality of the whole text by examining its introductory sentence(s) or verse(s):

> The first type of importance is controlled by the discourse topical framework which, in most stories, is unveiled in the course of the narration, but which sometimes is provided in a title, as is the case in the Genesis 22 story.[27]

Heimerdinger later adds:

> Nevertheless, it is possible to find the equivalent of Tomlin's thematic information connected to the goal of the discourse in stories which give clues as to their topical concerns through a brief statement or heading at the beginning. Such statements are not to be confused with headings used in news report which provide a gist or abstract of a text. Rather, they constitute what Brown and Yule call a "topic framework" and function as "a particularly powerful thematization device" (1983:139). This means that they list the topical elements around which the story is constructed. The title establishes the participants mentioned as the topical participants and the action as the topical action. The topicalization of specific entities in a story through a heading results in the readers focusing their attention on the elements in question because they create an expectation and are linked to the goal of the discourse.[28]

---

27. Heimerdinger, *Topic, Focus and Foreground*, 126.

28. Heimerdinger, *Topic, Focus and Foreground*, 105–06; Brown and Yule, *Discourse Analysis*, 75, 139. "From the content of the text the analyst can, in principle, determine what aspects of the context are explicitly reflected in the text as the formal record of the utterance. Those aspects of the context which are directly reflected in the text, and which need to be called upon to interpret the text, we shall refer to as *activated features of context* and suggest that they constitute the contextual framework within which the topic is constituted, that is, *the topic framework*. As a way of characterizing the type of feature which will be required in a topic framework, we shall examine a fragment of conversational discourse and try to determine what is being talked about . . . The 'title'

Analysis of the Balaam Text of Num 22–24

Although Heimerdinger's suggestion is different from mine, what is praiseworthy is that he places readers' attention on the first sentence or verse of a narrative.[29] In many Hebrew narratives in the OT, the beginning of the texts functions as a heading that contains the vital information regarding what is being talked about. The authors of the Hebrew narratives seem to use the first sentence/verse as the device to provide the topicality of the whole text. Thus, readers can recognize what the text is about and what will be unfolded through the entirety of a text. This allows readers to maintain focus on the message and intention of the text.

The Topical Verb(s) in the Heading of the Topic Frame in a Text

Understanding the function of the topical verb(s), that which provides the foundational idea of a text, is pivotal for the methodology of this study. First, the concept of the topical verb(s) identified by my methodology in

---

of a stretch of discourse should not be equated with 'the topic' but should be regarded as one possible expression of the topic. We now wish to propose that the best way of describing the function of the title of a discourse is as a particularly powerful thematisation device... The topic entity was thematised, or, to express the relationship more accurately, when we found the name of an individual thematised in the title of the text, we expected that individual to be the topic entity. This expectation-creating aspect of thematisation, especially in the form of a title, means that thematised elements provide not only a starting point around which what follows in the discourse is structured, but also a starting point which constrains our interpretation of what follows."

29. I insist that the key of the heading theory is verb(s), while he suggests the key of the heading is noun(s) which are mostly characters or participants in a given text. It is reasonable for Heimerdinger to suggest that there is the information on the topical participants and the topical actions in the beginning of a text, and the topical participants are more topical than the topical actions in the sense of the topical hierarchy (Heimerdinger insisted it in his book) with the example of Gen 22. However, the appropriateness of his suggestion is doubtful in the case of Num 22–24 because the topical participant in the beginning and first five verses of the text is Balak. According to the theory of Heimerdinger, Balak is the topical participant in the beginning of the text, and Balak should be treated the most important character in the whole text. But, the text of Num 22–24 is called "the Balaam story," not "the Balak story," by most commentaries, and the reading focuses on the character of Balaam. In my view, Heimerdinger's suggestion can be applicable in short and simple passages such as Gen 22, while it is not certain of the applicability in long and complicated passages such as Num 22–24. Interestingly, my suggestion, which is the verb's higher topicality than nouns (participants) in the beginning of text, is applicable and acceptable in both short and straightforward passages and long and complicated narratives.

this study is different from the concept of "keyword(s)."[30] Heimerdinger summarizes "the repetition of a keyword" by reference to Buber:

> Martin Buber was the first to identify an Old Hebrew narrative technique which he called *Leitwortstil* ("leading word style"), the use of keywords in Old Hebrew texts. *Leitwortstil* consists in the repetition of a characteristic word or root throughout a text and is used by the narrator to indicate the intended thrust or purpose of a story or an episode. The repetition of a word hammers home the intended message of the story to the hearer. Through it, the speaker ensures that the message of the story is correctly perceived. By tracing the repeated keyword of a text, the hearer opens the central meaning of the story. As such, the use of keywords belongs to the collection of evaluative devices. Buber believes that the repetition of keywords is the most effective way of making a point without disrupting the flow of the story.[31]

Moreover, topical verb(s) may repeatedly appear throughout an entire text. This feature of repetition seems to be similar to the repetition of keywords. However, the topical verb(s) is provided in the heading of a text as the lens for the reading of the entire text. Further, the only required part of speech is the verb, while a keyword can be located anywhere in the text, and is not limited in form to a specific part of speech, word, phrase, or clause.

---

30. Moyer, "Literary and Linguistic Studies in Sefer Bilʿam (Num 22–24)," 306, 307–19. He introduces the definition of "keyword" by relying on Buber. He also employs the explanation of Shimon Bar-Efrat when describing that "the threads of relationship drawn between the various repetitions of a given keyword provide a means of 'conveying the essential point directly,' and that such a keyword 'reveals the meaning and the implicit message of the narrative, without adversely affecting its pure artistic form in any way.'" But, his introduction of the term "keyword" is not enough to explain why a certain word should be treated as the keyword in a given text. He suggests the verb ראה as one of many keywords (קרא, עבר, קבב, ברך, נבט, שור, and יצב) in the Balaam story in his dissertation. Interestingly, he mentions only קבב (to curse) for the verb, even though ארר also was used to convey the same meaning in the text. It is also important to note that all the keywords he suggests are verbs to the exclusion of other repeated nouns and adverbs. He also does not recognize or prove the relationship between the keywords of the sense of sight and other keywords that create the implicit message for which he argues. Further, for the keyword of ראה, he suggests that ראה is the important keyword because it is a repeated keyword, and quotes Robert Alter: "To be more specific, Robert Alter referred to the verb ראה as 'the thematic keyword of this entire episode.'" Ironically, neither Alter nor Moyer mention why only ראה especially should be treated as the important keyword or the thematic keyword. The concept of the topical verb in this study can answer the question regarding the importance of the verb ראה.

31. Heimerdinger, *Topic, Focus and Foreground*, 246–47.

ANALYSIS OF THE BALAAM TEXT OF NUM 22–24

I will introduce Heimerdinger's basic idea on the topicality or the topical hierarchy in a narrative (text) in order to explain my methodology:

> In the ice-hockey game the goal of the reporting is to describe the action on ice. The verbal description of the game is organized by the extralinguistic activity of viewing the hockey game unfolding on ice and so the organization of the linguistic material will depend upon the salient features of the game on which the reporter's attention is focused: the puck and the players. The puck is topical: it is a centre of attention because its movement and its fate determine the outcome of the game. The players are topical: they are a centre of attention because they seek to control the puck and thus the outcome of the game. Of the two centres of attention, attention to the puck is more basic than attention to the players.[32] When a player takes control of the puck the two centres of attention coincide and reference to such a player becomes "more topical" than reference to the puck or another player without the puck. On this basis, a hierarchy of thematic information may be established:
>
> player in control of the puck > puck > player without puck > other
>
> The advantage of such a method is that the determination of levels of topicality takes place independently of the syntax.[33] It is linked to centres of attention in the extra-linguistic situation.[34]

In Heimerdinger's introduction above, action can be understood as a verb. One of the most critical purposes of the reporting of a hockey game is to announce the process by which the puck *moves* and its resultant effect of scoring in the game, in addition to announcing the condition of the ice, the number of spectators, introducing the players, commenting on the history of the two teams, etc. The shooting of the puck, however, is the most important factor, because it effects a score in the game. Thus, it is meaningful to trace the movement of the puck in the game. To follow the puck is to examine the topical verb(s) to recognize the topicality in a text and to confirm the message and the intention of a text. Further, although someone

---

32. Through this statement Heimerdinger already recognizes the fundamental importance of the verb where he says, "it [the puck] is a center of attention because [of] its *movement*." Heimerdinger, *Topic, Focus and Foreground*, 105. Emphasis mine.

33. I agree with Heimerdinger on this point, and thus will examine the text from the broadest perspective, not limiting myself to an analysis of the syntax. I consider various elements such as the literary expression, the style, and the structure of the text, as well as the syntactic features in my efforts to find the message and the intention of the text.

34. Heimerdinger, *Topic, Focus and Foregrounding*, 105.

Who Is the True Seer Driven by God?

can insist that from the beginning of the game the audience's eyes would be focused on the player who is in control of the puck, in fact, the reason that the player has the attention of the audience is that the player will soon move the puck. This is the fundamental reason to insist that verb(s) in the heading has the topicality in a text.

Although Heimerdinger does not reject the role and importance of verbs in Hebrew narratives, he limits his discussion of them to being one of many elements comprising the topical frame in the heading, which is the beginning of a narrative. Heimerdinger insists that referents or subjects that are not verbs have the highest topical importance in a narrative.[35] However, I suggest that the topicality of the verb in the heading should be observed through the development of the sub-topical verbs through the entire narrative.

In the introduction of a hierarchy of thematic information above, Heimerdinger listed the thematic informational elements in order of hierarchy such as 1. Player in control of the puck, 2. Puck, 3. Player without puck, 4. Other. However, I point out the weakness of Heimerdinger's list. Heimerdinger suggested that the player in control of the puck has the highest topicality in the hierarchy. Is it true? Then, which one is more topical between the status of a player having the puck and the state of the puck moving to any direction toward ultimate goal? The primary concern of the audience in the hockey game is not to watch a player who has the puck, but to follow the puck going toward the goal net. Therefore, I suggest the order in the list be changed to the following: "the moving puck > player moving/shooting the puck > player not moving or shooting the puck > other."

Likewise, the topical verb(s) in the heading of a text has the highest topicality because it identifies not only the general subject of the text, but also the direction of the plot of the narrative. The topical verb functions like a backbone, and there are many elements (sub-topical verb[s], the topically-related verbs, key phrases, etc.) working as flesh to develop the body of a text. Thus, all elements should be examined to confirm the main plot and message of a text, but the topical verb(s) is the fundamental element that affirms what the text is "about." Heimerdinger properly states that the verb functions as the topical action at the beginning of a text; however, the role of the verb should not be limited to the action at the beginning of a text. Instead, the function of the topical verb must be examined throughout the

---

35. Heimerdinger, *Topic, Focus and Foregrounding*, 106, 108. Heimerdinger insists that "the main topical participant is Actor."

Analysis of the Balaam Text of Num 22–24

whole text due to how it contributes to the formation of the storyline, the message and the intention of the text.

The Combination of the Topical Verb + Noun (Subject/Character)

As mentioned above, "shooting" and "player moving/shooting of the puck" are more important than "player not moving/shooting of the puck" and "other elements" in an ice hockey game. Likewise, topical verb and noun (character) coming with the verb are crucial to understand the topicality in a text. In the combination of the topical verb + noun, the noun includes basically subject/character and extensively object. The participations of the subjects and objects around the topical verb(s) and topically-related verbs manifest the topicality and the relationship between the topical verb(s) and topically-related verbs in a text. I will show the example in the Balaam story in detail later.

The Use of the Topical Verb(s) in Other Texts of the OT

THE PENTATEUCH (GEN 22:1–19)[36]

The verb נסה (to test) in 22:1 is the key verb in the background information. The topical verbs are לקח (to take) and עלה (to present a sacrifice at the altar: *hiphil*)[37], and the combination of the topical verbs + noun (character) is that Abraham takes and brings (his son [for a burnt offering]). Thus, this narrative should be read in light of both the background information that God tests Abraham and the topical frame of Abraham taking and bringing his son for a burnt offering. Under the control of the topicality through the

---

36. Safren, "Balaam and Abraham," 105–13. Although Safren does not come to an obvious conclusion from the comparison between Num 22:22–35 and Gen 22:1–19, he introduces meaningful parallels between the two narratives. He mentions similarities of the keywords ("see" and "sword") as well as setting, characters, and plot between the two narratives: "a journey by ass," "an angel revealing himself to the protagonist at the climax of the plot (Gen 22:11; Num 22:31)," and "both Abraham and Balaam are 'prophets' (Gen 20:7 and Balaam's mantic powers from his oracles)." He also suggests stylistic similarities between the two narratives as below:

(1) "And Balaam rose in the morning and saddled his ass (Num 22:21)."
"And Abraham rose early in the morning and saddled his ass (Gen 22:3)."
(2) "and he was riding on his ass and his two servants with him (Num 22:22)."
"and he saddled his ass and he took his two servants with him (Gen 22:3)."

37. "עלה," *HALOT*, 1:830.

topical frame with the topical verbs, the characters related to the topicality in the narrative become topical regarding the message of the narrative.

The topical verbs לקח and עלה appear repeatedly in verses 3, 6, 7/8 (לְעֹלָה: for burnt offering [from the same root of the verb]), 10 (עלה), and 13. It shows that the topicality through the topical verb is predominant in the story. The sub-topical verbs, חוה (to worship) and בנה (to build [the altar]), ערך (to arrange [the trees]), עקד (to bind [Isaac his son]), שים (to put [him on the altar]) share the same meaning with the topical verbs. Through the supportive work of the sub-topical verbs, the topicality of the topical verbs is introduced and developed in detail.

The first topically-related verb is ראה (to see) because the verb is topically related to the topical verb and occurs repeatedly in the crucial scenes. The main characters' seeing is deeply connected to the action of "offering (the topical verbs)" in the important scenes of the story. The verb occurs with the temporal adverb (בַּיּוֹם הַשְּׁלִישִׁי, on the third day) which draws readers' attention in verse 4: "Abraham lifted up his eyes and saw the place from afar." After the verse, this verb repeatedly appears in verses 8 ("God sees [will see] for himself the lamb for a burnt offering"), 13 ("Abraham lifted up his eyes and saw") and 14 ("Abraham called the name of that place, 'the Lord sees [will see]'"). The second topically-related verb is ברך (to bless) because the verb is also topically related and occurs in the important concluding scene. The verb is conceptually connected to the topical verb regarding the purpose and result of the offering: Abraham's offering is to receive the blessing from the Lord for the result of his obedience.

Since the heading, the combination of the topical verbs (the sub-topical and topically-related verbs) and nouns (the characters) shows that the topical main characters are the Lord, Abraham, Isaac, and the angel of the Lord. Among them, the Lord and Abraham are the most important topical characters as the giver and receiver (who takes action) around the topicality. As the result, the topicality of the story shows the message through the works of the topical verbs (Abraham's "sacrificing" [his son]) and the topically-related verbs ("seeing" and "blessing"). God commands Abraham to slaughter/sacrifice his son, sees what Abraham sees, and blesses him as the result of the test. Finally, Abraham becomes God's tool delivering the blessing toward all the nations of the earth through his offspring.

Analysis of the Balaam Text of Num 22–24

Historical Books (2 Sam 11:1–12:25)

In this passage, verse 1 provides the informational background beginning with "vayhi" and the heading beginning with 11:1 (וַיִּשְׁחֹת֖וּb). The verbs שלח (to send), שחת (to destroy/corrupt), and ישב (to dwell/remain) in 11:1b and 11:1c are the topical verbs. The combination of the topical verbs + noun (character) is that David sends Joab, his servants, and all Israel out to battle and remains at Jerusalem. Thus, this narrative should be read in light of both the background information that it is the year when kings go out to battle and the topical frame of David sending his men of Israel out to battle and remaining at Jerusalem. Under the control of the topicality through the topical frame with the topical verbs, the characters related to the topicality in the narrative become topical regarding the message of the narrative.

The primary topical character of the topical verbs is David because he is active doer of the verbs even though the subjects of the topical verb שחת are Joab, David's servants, and all Israel. Through the whole narrative, the topical verb שחת is prominent because it is developed to the sub-topical verb מות (to die) which is widely distributed throughout the narrative. The verb שחת can be synonymous with the verb מות in this narrative because מות was used in the context of "killing men" with sword in other passages of the OT: Judg 20:25, 35.

The sub-topical verb מות appear repeatedly in 11:15, 17, 21, 24, 26; 12:5, 13, 14, 18, 19, 21, and 23. It shows that the topicality through the topical and sub-topical verb is predominant in the narrative. Through the supportive work of the sub-topical verb, the topicality of the topical verb is introduced and developed in detail.

Since the heading, the combination of the topical verb (the sub-topical verb) and nouns (characters) shows that the topical characters are David, Uriah, Bathsheba, Nathan, and David's child. Among them, David is the most important topical character as the evildoer and receiver of the blame for the evildoing around the topicality. The sub-topical verb is relevant to David's evildoing. Further, "dying" reveals what David did for the evil thing in the climax of the narrative. According to the topicality through the topical verb and the sub-topical verb, the message of this narrative is as follows: (1) David sends his men of Israel out to battle to destroy the Ammonites and remains at Jerusalem; (2) David sees a woman (Bathsheba) and does the evil thing (making her husband, Uriah, die); (3) Nathan rebukes David who despised the word of the Lord to do evil thing (killing Uriah and taking his wife); (4) The child, who is born to David, dies because of David's evildoing; (5) David earns a baby, who is called Solomon (Jedidiah), from Bathsheba.

Conclusion

The purpose of this section is to show that my methodology's emphasis on the connection between the topical verb(s) and the coherence, message, and intention of a text is not limited to the Balaam story in Num 22–24, but can be applied to other passages in the OT. In some passages the topical verb(s) appear only once in the heading of the text, while in others, such as Num 22–24, the topical verb(s) appear repeatedly throughout the text after first appearing in the heading. My suggested methodology could be applied to narrative passages and mixed passages of prose and poetry, and is useful for predicting outcomes in complicated and long passages in addition to short and straightforward passages in the OT.

The Topical Verb(s) and the Development of Topicality in a Text

Sub-Topical Verb(s)

The topical verb(s) is the backbone that shapes the topicality of the main storyline, message, and the intention of a text. But, it cooperates with other verbs to maintain the topicality throughout a text. The sub-topical verb is synonymous with the topical verb(s) in the heading. The sub-topical verb(s), maintaining the concept of the topical verb(s), helps to develop the topicality of the whole text. For the purpose of preserving topicality, the sub-topical verb(s) also works with topically-related verbs and other verbs. Finally, it is possible to create a hierarchy among the verbs, which is typically arranged from the topical verb(s), to the sub-topical verb(s), to the topically-related verbs, and finally to other verbs. For the Balaam story in Num 22–24, the topical verb is ראה (to see), and the sub-topical verbs are חזה (to see), גלה (to uncover [the eyes]), שתמ (to be opened [the eyes]), שור (to behold), and נבט (to observe). The topically-related verbs are דבר (to speak)/עשׂה (to do)/ברך (to bless)/ארר (to curse)/קבב (to curse), הרג (to slay)/זבח (to slaughter)/מות (to die)/עלה (to sacrifice).

ANALYSIS OF THE BALAAM TEXT OF NUM 22–24

The Topical Verb(s) and Repetition/Pattern/Structure (the Topically-Related Verbs) in a Text

In order to develop the topicality of a text, some words, phrases, or clauses can be repeated throughout the whole text.[38] The objects of repetition that form the topicality are the topical verb(s), the sub-topical verb(s), the topically-related verbs, and topic-related words/phrases/clauses. In the Balaam story in Num 22–24, the topical verb(s) itself repeatedly occurs from the beginning to the end of the text, and the synonymous sub-topical verbs that appear in the whole text should be understood as essentially repeating the topical verb. Other repeated words/phrases/clauses related to the topicality also are connected to the topical verb. Repetition is the primary device that conveys the topicality originating from the topical verb.[39]

Alter helpfully delineates the use of repetition in the Hebrew narratives.[40] According to Alter, repetition is one of the most critical literary

---

38. Walsh, *Style and Structure*, 7–10. "Repetition is the most common formal device for organizing a literary unit in biblical Hebrew prose. Repetition, of course, can serve many literary functions in a prose text: repeated words or themes (e.g., keywords or leitmotifs) can unify a passage, create emphasis, or delay action and create suspense . . . In principle, repetition can involve any element, from phonemes (i.e., sounds: alliteration, assonance, and the like) to large, thematically coherent units. In practice, phonemic repetition is more typical of poetry than of prose. At particularly significant junctures, however, Hebrew narrative prose may take on more properly prosodic characteristics such as balance, parallelism, rhythm, and sound patterning, Phonemic repetition, then, does occur in prose, but as an organizing device it is relatively rare; only a few examples will figure in the discussions that follow . . . Repetitions of conceptually significant words (e.g., nouns, verbs) are more noticeable than those of ordinary conjunctions, prepositions, and the like . . . Thematic or conceptual repetition, i.e., repetition that involves similarity of thought without any similarity of language, is more difficult to identify and assess. That it occurs is beyond question. The use of stereotyped word pairs (e.g., 'justice' and 'righteousness'; 'heaven' and 'earth') is one example; synonymous and antithetic parallelism in Hebrew poetry is another. But identification of a structure solely or primarily on the basis of conceptual repetition runs the risk of relying too heavily on subjective judgment to be convincing. Where thematic repetition involves stereotyped word pairs attested elsewhere in the Hebrew Bible the risk is lessened. Where it does not, as is frequently the case in large-scale structures, other, more objectively demonstrable repeated elements are essential to support the structural analysis."

39. Provan et al., *A Biblical History of Israel*, 91–93. "OT narratives are scenic . . . OT narratives are subtle . . . OT narratives are succinct . . . They use all manner of repetitions to great advantage—words and word stems (i.e., *Leitworte*), motifs, similar situations (sometimes called 'type-scenes' or 'stock situations'), and the like. The effect of repetition is often to underscore a central theme or concern in a narrative."

40. Alter, *The Art of Biblical Narrative*, 223. "The repetition of single words or brief

devices because it reveals a thematic significance. He treats it as a keyword that delivers the messages and theological meanings within a story. Furthermore, I suggest that repetition in the sense of a keyword also could include the connection to the topicality originating from the topical verb(s), the sub-topical verbs, the topically-related verbs, and other cooperative elements to form and develop the topicality through the whole text.

Regular repetitions of the topical verb(s) or other elements related to the topicality can create and disclose patterns within a given text. Pattern also reveals the structure of the text. These literary devices are useful to manifest the message and the intention of the text systematically. The features of the pattern and structure of a text also aid readers to recognize what the text is saying and what the text means.[41]

For example, the purpose of the development of the topically-related verb דבר (to speak) from the topical verb ראה (to see) in the phrase "speak only the word that I tell you" is to let Balaam, who functions as God's tool, know and deliver what God willingly wants to disclose from his mind. This thematic phrase occurs repeatedly primarily at the end of each episode:

---

phrases often exhibits a frequency, a saliency, and a thematic significance quite unlike what we may be accustomed to from other narrative traditions. The one most prominent device involving the repetition of single words is the use of the *Leitwort*, the thematic keyword, as a way of enunciating and developing the moral, historical, psychological, or theological meanings of the story. What befalls the protagonist of the biblical tale is emphatically punctuated by significance, and the *Leitwort* is a principal means of punctuation. Where the narration so abundantly encourages us to expect this sort of repetition, on occasion the avoidance of repetition, whether through substitution of a synonym or of a wholly divergent word or phrase for the anticipated recurrence, may also be particularly revealing. Repeated words may be relatively abstract, like 'blessing' in Genesis, and so point toward a thematic idea, or they may be entirely concrete, like 'stones' in the Jacob story, and so serve to carry forward narrative motifs that do not have one clear thematic significance."

41. Walsh, *Style and Structure*, 8–9. Walsh introduces the role of patterns and structures in detail: "Correspondence between subunits is effected by repeated elements, and the pattern is schematized by using letters to refer to each subunit: ABCA′B′C′ or ABCDC′B′A′, for instance. The possible variations of symmetrical patterning afford the biblical Hebrew narrator a flexible tool not only for integrating and organizing a literary unit, but for directing the reader's interpretive attention as well. The interpretive impact is twofold. First, structural units are often thematic units (like paragraphs in English prose) or dramatic ones (like scenes). To the degree that symmetrical patterning enables us to discern the extent and limits of a literary unit it can provide clues to the thematic structure of the passage. Second, as we shall see, different forms of symmetry tend toward different interpretive dynamics: reinforcement and intensification, comparison, contrast reversal, and so forth . . . It is more common in prose for repeated roots, words, word pairs, and whole phrases to appear as structuring elements."

Analysis of the Balaam Text of Num 22–24

22:18, 20 (episode 3); 22:35 (episode 5); 22:38 (episode 6); 23:12 (episode 7); 23:26 (episode 8); 24:13, 14 (episode 9). This pattern of repetition exposes the intention of the author in the text systematically.

Considering the structure of Num 22–24, it seems natural to divide the Balaam story into nine episodes according to changes in the locations, characters, and scenes. According to the topical verb, the sub-topical verbs, the related verbs, and other topically-related elements, the nine episodes form a structure of concentric symmetry. This structure portrays an intense relationship between God, Balaam, and Balak. I will introduce it in detail in the next section.

The Topical Verb(s) and the Main Characters in the Balaam Story of Num 22–24

The topical verb(s) are the most important elements to reveal the topicality of a text. However, the combination of "the topical verb + noun (subject/character)" should not go unheeded because the topicality of a text is disclosed and conveyed through the cooperative work of the characters effectively. The characters who participate in the work of the topical verb are called "topical character(s)."

For the topicality of nouns (main characters), as I have mentioned on pages 33–37, I disagree with the following hierarchical suggestion of Heimerdinger: "player in control of the puck > puck > player without puck > other." Rather, I suggest an ordering of "shoot > player moving/shooting of the puck > player not moving or shooting the puck > other" because of the importance of the conveyance of thematic information. According to my suggestion, shooting (verb) assumes the highest degree of topicality in the heading, while players (participants) are not guaranteed to be topical. Although certain participants in the heading can be treated as topical entities, they could be low hierarchically among other participants in the whole story. That is, the participants occurring in the heading have tentative topicality, but as the story proceeds, according to their relationship with the topical verb(s), other participants may take that position. Therefore, the highest degree of topical entities among participants (main characters) in a story is not determined immediately and automatically in the heading but should be examined through the whole story. In some stories, such as Gen 22:1–19, the topical participants (main characters) are introduced in the heading and keep their topicality until the end of the story, while in other

Who Is the True Seer Driven by God?

accounts, such as Num 22–24, the highest topical participants are revealed after the heading. The author controls the plan regarding the arrangement of the highest topical characters, topically-related characters, and non-topical characters.

In the case of the Balaam story in Num 22–24, in the heading the topical verb is ראה (to see) and the topical participant (character) is Balak. Here, Balak receives the temporal topicality as a character who is related to the topical verb, ראה. Afterward, Balaam becomes a higher topical character than Balak. The reason that Balaam's topicality is higher than that of Balak is that Balaam occurs more frequently connected to the topical verb and takes the action of the topical verb. Ultimately, the highest topical character is God, not Balaam or Balak, because God is the character closest to the topical verb, ראה. God originates and controls the action of the topical verb, ראה, in the climactic episode 5. In the episode, God appears, with the first sub-topical verb (גלה, "to uncover [Balaam's eyes]"), as the most important topical character who makes Balaam his tool for the mission of "seeing."[42] God makes Balaam see what he should see, but God does not work for Balak, who longed to see what he wanted to see.[43] Therefore, the hierarchical order from highest to lowest is God, Balaam, and Balak.

As mentioned previously, this kind of complicated hierarchical system of topical participants might not show the highest degree of the topical participant in the heading. For example, Jephthah does not appear in the heading of his story (Judg 10:6–12:7), and Ruth does not occur in the heading of hers (Ruth 1–4). However, it is more typical for shorter and

---

42. The Lord could be treated as the highest topical character not because he is always the subject of the topical verb in the narrative, but because he is the subject of the first sub-topical verb in the climactic episode 5 in which the cooperative work of the first sub-topical verb and topically-related verbs reveals the topicality in detail. In this episode, the Lord is introduced as the character who is able to control Balaam's vision.

43. The narrative of the first tells us what Balak sees; he *actually* sees what Israel had done to the Amorites (not what the Lord had done to the Amorites) in 22:2. Balak (and Balaam) also could see a fraction of the people (Israel) in 22:41. In the narrative parts, Balak is introduced as the character who is able to see Israel and respond to the fear and dread from Israel. Later, in the poetic parts, Balak is presented as the character who is interested in God and his message through Balaam's oracles. It means that Balak does not have the access to the topicality of "seeing" shared by God and Balaam in the first half of the Balaam story, even though Balak seems to be a temporal topical character in the heading. Balak does not appear as the subject of the topical and sub-topical verbs except for only 22:2 in the whole Balaam story. The fact that the topicality of "seeing" is shared by mainly God and Balaam shows that Balak is incidental in the hierarchical order regarding the topicality of "seeing."

simpler stories to have a simpler hierarchy of topical participants, introducing the highest degree of topical participants (characters) directly in the heading to more quickly unfold the plot. What is most important, thus, is a) that the verb(s) occurring in the head (distinguished from the background information) carry the topicality of the whole story, and b) that the topical verb(s) influence the topicality of the participants (characters) and their topical hierarchy; therefore, the combination of "the topical verb(s) + subjects/participants/characters" should be considered as important for tracing the topicality of a text.

Conclusion

The selected studies of Heimerdinger above are helpful for outlining my methodology. The primary difference between Heimerdinger's methodology and my own regarding topicality is that topical entities (nouns) are essential for Heimerdinger, while I consider verbs to be the central elements of topicality throughout an entire text.[44]

In this section, I have insisted that the verb(s) occurring in the first sentence (verse) of the heading establish the topical framework that conveys the intention or the message of a text. Accordingly, regular occurrences of the topical verb(s) and the related sub-topical verbs in the entire text serve to cohere and participate in the implied author's intended message in the text. The grasping of the topical and the sub-topical verb(s) are also a useful tool for discerning the structure of a text. With this tool, it is possible to appreciate the implied author's writing style, the way the message is delivered, and the literary techniques used to express the intention. This methodology was derived from a careful reading of the Balaam story in Num 22–24 and can be applied to other OT passages.

---

44. Heimerdinger, *Topic, Focus and Foreground*, 107. "The verb establishes a general controlling framework. It describes how things are going to develop in the discourse and any possible entity (other participants, props, objects, place) associated with the notion of 'test' must be examined in terms of linguistic encoding." Heimerdinger also is interested in the combination of verb + (nominal) entity in the heading. However, Heimerdinger focuses more on the nominal entity or character, while I treat the verb as more important.

Who Is the True Seer Driven by God?
An Analysis of the Text of the Balaam Story in Num 22–24

Introduction

In this section, I will delimitate the text of the Balaam story in Num 22–24 and analyze it. In the analysis of the text, I will show Hebrew and English texts organized by the verbal phrases and the episodes. Particularly, I will suggest that the flow, message, and intention of the story are controlled by the systematic interrelationship of the topical verb, the sub-topical verbs, the topically-related verbs, and the topically-related main characters so that they develop the topicality, and form the pattern, structure, and main topic in each episode and the whole story.

Delimitation of the Text of the Balaam Story in Num 22–24

Introduction

An independent unit of a text could be delimitated by many elements, such as textual traditions, literary tools and contexts, linguistic devices, etc. According to Heimerdinger, there are fundamental and obvious devices for the delimitation of a text: boundary markers, adverbial phrases of location or time, the dispersing of participants or the introduction of a new cast of participants, a noun as an explicit subject or a summary statement, and events.[45] With these literary devices, I will introduce some ways to delimitate the Balaam story in Num 22–24 to analyze the well-woven story.[46]

It is important to discuss whether the first verse in the beginning of the Balaam text in Num 22–24 should be Num 22:1 or Num 22:2, because the topical verb that determines the message and intention of a text is located in the heading, which is typically the first verse or sentence of a textual unit. Accordingly, in order to find the topical verb of the Balaam text, we must

---

45. Heimerdinger, *Topic, Focus and Foreground*, 108–09. Although Heimerdinger introduces these devices in the sense of determining the topical importance of entities, they can be treated as important literary devices for delimitating a text.

46. Ashley, *The Book of Numbers*, 433; Cole, *Numbers*, 363–64, 371. Milgrom suggests that "the poetic oracles and the narrative were originally independent of each other, discrete epics on the same theme, which fused as a later date by a single editorial hand. However, even were this so, the fusion is so thoroughgoing and skillful that the original seams are no longer visible: The redaction is a new artistic creation" (Milgrom, *Numbers*, 468). Cf. Wenham, *Numbers*, 58. On the specific question of the unity of the Balaam pericope, see, e.g., Clark, "Balaam's Ass: Suture or Structure?" 137–44.

Analysis of the Balaam Text of Num 22–24

first delimit the text unit. Though scholars are divided, I will describe below my reasoning for accepting Num 22:2 as the heading for Num 22–24.[47]

The Textual Tradition of Masorah

In the Masoretic text, the Pentateuch utilizes division signs for religious or liturgical readings. The major signs are "Sop Pasuq" (end of verse) which end a verse, "פ, Petuha/ס, Setuma" (open/closed), which are paragraph markings, and "Seder/Parashiyyot," which are liturgical division.[48] The book of Numbers has thirty-three Sedarim and nine Parashiyyot.[49] The twentieth Seder and the sixth Parash separate 22:1 and 22:2. Furthermore, a ס also stands between the two verses. That is, the three division signs regarding the paragraph marking and the liturgical reading of ס, Seder, and Parashiyyot are located between 22:1 and 22:2. According to this Masoretic division sign, it is obvious that the verses of Num 22:1 and 22:2 are divided by the Masoretic textual tradition following the Palestinian and Babylonian

---

47. Cf. Olson, *Numbers*; Budd, *Numbers*; Knierim and Coats, *Numbers*; and Bailey insist that 22:1 opens the Balaam story, while Levine, Milgrom, van Seters, Childs, and Ashley suggest that 22:2 opens the Balaam story. While there are various reasons for the advocates insisting that Num 22:1 should be included in the Balaam text of Num 22–24, source criticism scholars mostly treat Num 22:1 as an insertion from the P source, and prefer to detach it from Num 22:2 and connect it to the previous verse, 21:35.

48. Kelley et al., *The Masorah of Biblia Hebraica Stuttgartensia*, 155. "Seder" literally means "order, sequence"; "This was the name assigned to the sections into which the Torah was divided for the Sabbath readings in the synagogues. In Palestine, where the custom was to complete the reading in three to three and a half years, the Torah was divided into 154 or 167 sedarim. BHS has 167 Torah sedarim." For setuma and petuha, "long before the introduction of chapter divisions, the entire Bible was divided on the basis of content into short paragraphs, also known as parashiyyot. A paragraph could be either 'open' (petuha) or 'closed' (setuma) . . . An *s* in the body of the text indicates that the following paragraph is closed; a *p* indicates that it is open." Cf. Scott, *A Simplified Guide to BHS*, 1–2; for parashah: "These abbreviations divide the Pentateuch into fifty-four lessons. The parashiyyot are longer sections similar in function to the sedarim." While the divisions of the seder are associated with the Palestinian tradition, the divisions of the parashah are associated with the Babylonian tradition.

49. The divisions by Seder in the book of Numbers are: 1 (Num 1:1), 2 (2:1), 3 (3:1), 4 (4:17), 5 (5:11), 6 (6:1), 7 (6:22), 8 (7:48), 9 (8:1), 10 (10:1), 11 (11:16), 12 (11:23), 13 (13:1), 14 (14:11), 15 (15:1), 16 (16:1), 17 (17:16), 18 (19:1), 19 (20:14), 20 (22:2), 21 (23:10), 22 (25:1), 23 (25:10), 24 (26:52), 25 (27:15), 26 (28:26), 27 (30:2), 28 (31:1), 29 (31:25), 30 (32:1), 31 (33:1), 32 (34:1), 33 (35:9); The divisions by Parash in the book of Numbers include: 1 (Num 4:21), 2 (8:1), 3 (13:1), 4 (16:1), 5 (19:1), 6 (22:2), 7 (25:10), 8 (30:2), 9 (33:1).

tradition of textual reading. The signs, ס located before Num 22:2 and פ after Num 24:25, show that the text of the Balaam story is set from Num 22:2 to Num 24:25.

According to the divisions of Seder and Parashiyyot, the Balaam text of Num 22–24 can be divided as 22:2–23:9 and 23:10–24:25 (Seder) or 22:2–25:9 (Parash). The two divisions of Seder and the one Parash both suggest that the reading of the Balaam story should begin from verse 2 of chapter 22, even though they indicate different final verses for each reading. Accordingly, the two traditions of division contained in the Masoretic text seem to support beginning the Balaam story at Num 22:2.

The Division of Paragraphs by the Literary/Linguistic Features

As Brevard Childs asserts, it is more suitable to analyze a biblical text by the linguistic features of the final form of a text than to rely on source critical methods when examining its literary aspects.[50] Linguistic features indicate that it is more natural to view Num 22:1 as the conclusion of the previous paragraph, a narrative focused on Israel's war campaigning, than to propose it as the beginning verse of the Balaam text.[51] The expression "the people of Israel camped in the plains of Moab" occurs in Num 22:1. The verbal expression of "to camp" has the form of the combination of חנה(ו) . . . נסע (to set out . . . and to camp) in Hebrew. This form occurs five times in Num 21:10–22:1 to make a distinction between the passage of Num 21:10–22:1 and its surrounding paragraphs. The unit of 21:10–22:1 introducing Israel's journey seems to use the linguistic feature of חנה(ו) . . . נסע to signify the beginning and the end of the independent unit, namely Israel's campaign narrative.[52] Accordingly, it seems to be reasonable to reckon Num 22:2 as the beginning of a new unit, the Balaam story.

50. Childs, *Introduction to the Old Testament as Scripture*, 73.

51. Ashley, *The Book of Numbers*, 430–31. Ashley also treats Num 22:1 as the verse describing the end of Israel's journey in the book of Numbers. He further points out that the verbal expression of "to camp" in 22:1 occurs in 21:10–11. It seems to support the logic that 22:1 belongs to the previous paragraph rather than begins a new paragraph.

52. In examining other uses of the expression of "חנה . . . נסע" in the book of Numbers to ascertain whether it was used to signify the conclusion of a unit, story, or narrative, the form of "חנה . . . נסע" occurs in three narratives: in the end of the story of Miriam and Aaron opposing Moses (Num 12:16), in the beginning and the end of the narrative that Israel possessed the east side of the Jordan (21:10, 11, 12, 13, and 22:1), and the recounting of Israel's journey (33:5–37, 41–48). The form in Num 12:16 shows

Analysis of the Balaam Text of Num 22–24

The suggestion that Num 22:2 is the beginning of a new passage is also supported by the different subjects of the co-texts. The subjects of Num 22:1 and 25:1 are Israel and the people of Israel, while the external subjects of Num 22:2–24:25 are Balaam and Balak.[53] Thus, the Balaam story in Num 22:2–24:25 is distinguished from its co-texts, which have the subject of Israel. Accordingly, Num 22:1 should be treated as the concluding description of the final itinerary of Israel's possession of the east side of the Jordan, while Num 24:25 could be considered the end of the Balaam story.

Num 22:1 provides the background information of the Balaam story, which begins at Num 22:2, and functions as the conclusion of chapter 21. The Balaam story begins with Balak's response to the fact that Israel is encamped in the plain of Moab. However, Num 22:1 cannot function as the heading of the Balaam story because Num 22:1 has Israel as its subject; from Num 22:2, Israel no longer appears as the subject.

The Hebrew Text of the Balaam Story

(The Balaam Story: Num 22:2–24:25)[54]

22:2 וַיַּרְא בָּלָק בֶּן־צִפּוֹר אֵת כָּל־אֲשֶׁר־עָשָׂה יִשְׂרָאֵל לָאֱמֹרִי׃

3 וַיָּגָר מוֹאָב מִפְּנֵי הָעָם מְאֹד כִּי רַב־הוּא
וַיָּקָץ מוֹאָב מִפְּנֵי בְּנֵי יִשְׂרָאֵל׃

4 וַיֹּאמֶר מוֹאָב אֶל־זִקְנֵי מִדְיָן
עַתָּה יְלַחֲכוּ הַקָּהָל אֶת־כָּל־סְבִיבֹתֵינוּ
כִּלְחֹךְ הַשּׁוֹר אֵת יֶרֶק הַשָּׂדֶה
וּבָלָק בֶּן־צִפּוֹר מֶלֶךְ לְמוֹאָב בָּעֵת הַהִוא׃

5 וַיִּשְׁלַח מַלְאָכִים אֶל־בִּלְעָם בֶּן־בְּעֹר פְּתוֹרָה
אֲשֶׁר עַל־הַנָּהָר אֶרֶץ בְּנֵי־עַמּוֹ לִקְרֹא־לוֹ
לֵאמֹר הִנֵּה עַם יָצָא מִמִּצְרַיִם
הִנֵּה כִסָּה אֶת־עֵין הָאָרֶץ

---

obviously that it concludes the narrative, and the bundle of the form in Num 33:5–37 and 33:41–48 shaped the distinctive recounting narrative of Israel's journey.

53. Israel is the subject in Num 21:31–22:1.

54. The indentation of each line in the Balaam text of Num 22:2–24:25 shows the demarcation by the units of clause. It reflects the appearance of every kind of verb including the immanent verbs "to be."

Who Is the True Seer Driven by God?

וְהוּא יֹשֵׁב מִמֻּלִי:
6 וְעַתָּה לְכָה־נָּא אָרָה־לִּי אֶת־הָעָם הַזֶּה
כִּי־עָצוּם הוּא מִמֶּנִּי
אוּלַי אוּכַל נַכֶּה־בּוֹ וַאֲגָרְשֶׁנּוּ מִן־הָאָרֶץ
כִּי יָדַעְתִּי אֵת אֲשֶׁר־תְּבָרֵךְ מְבֹרָךְ
וַאֲשֶׁר תָּאֹר יוּאָר:
7 וַיֵּלְכוּ זִקְנֵי מוֹאָב וְזִקְנֵי מִדְיָן וּקְסָמִים בְּיָדָם
וַיָּבֹאוּ אֶל־בִּלְעָם
וַיְדַבְּרוּ אֵלָיו דִּבְרֵי בָלָק:
8 וַיֹּאמֶר אֲלֵיהֶם
לִינוּ פֹה הַלַּיְלָה
וַהֲשִׁבֹתִי אֶתְכֶם דָּבָר
כַּאֲשֶׁר יְדַבֵּר יְהוָה אֵלָי
וַיֵּשְׁבוּ שָׂרֵי־מוֹאָב עִם־בִּלְעָם:
9 וַיָּבֹא אֱלֹהִים אֶל־בִּלְעָם
וַיֹּאמֶר מִי הָאֲנָשִׁים הָאֵלֶּה עִמָּךְ:
10 וַיֹּאמֶר בִּלְעָם אֶל־הָאֱלֹהִים
בָּלָק בֶּן־צִפֹּר מֶלֶךְ מוֹאָב שָׁלַח אֵלָי:
11 הִנֵּה הָעָם הַיֹּצֵא מִמִּצְרַיִם
וַיְכַס אֶת־עֵין הָאָרֶץ
עַתָּה לְכָה קָבָה־לִּי אֹתוֹ
אוּלַי אוּכַל לְהִלָּחֶם בּוֹ וְגֵרַשְׁתִּיו:
12 וַיֹּאמֶר אֱלֹהִים אֶל־בִּלְעָם
לֹא תֵלֵךְ עִמָּהֶם
לֹא תָאֹר אֶת־הָעָם
כִּי בָרוּךְ הוּא:
13 וַיָּקָם בִּלְעָם בַּבֹּקֶר
וַיֹּאמֶר אֶל־שָׂרֵי בָלָק
לְכוּ אֶל־אַרְצְכֶם
כִּי מֵאֵן יְהוָה לְתִתִּי לַהֲלֹךְ עִמָּכֶם:
14 וַיָּקוּמוּ שָׂרֵי מוֹאָב
וַיָּבֹאוּ אֶל־בָּלָק
וַיֹּאמְרוּ
מֵאֵן בִּלְעָם הֲלֹךְ עִמָּנוּ:
15 וַיֹּסֶף עוֹד בָּלָק שְׁלֹחַ שָׂרִים רַבִּים וְנִכְבָּדִים מֵאֵלֶּה:

Analysis of the Balaam Text of Num 22–24

16 וַיָּבֹ֖אוּ אֶל־בִּלְעָ֑ם
וַיֹּ֣אמְרוּ ל֗וֹ
כֹּ֤ה אָמַר֙ בָּלָ֣ק בֶּן־צִפּ֔וֹר
אַל־נָ֥א תִמָּנַ֖ע מֵהֲלֹ֥ךְ אֵלָֽי׃
17 כִּֽי־כַבֵּ֤ד אֲכַבֶּדְךָ֙ מְאֹ֔ד
וְכֹ֛ל אֲשֶׁר־תֹּאמַ֥ר אֵלַ֖י אֶֽעֱשֶׂ֑ה
וּלְכָה־נָּא֙ קָֽבָה־לִּ֔י אֵ֖ת הָעָ֥ם הַזֶּֽה׃
18 וַיַּ֣עַן בִּלְעָ֗ם
וַיֹּ֙אמֶר֙ אֶל־עַבְדֵ֣י בָלָ֔ק
אִם־יִתֶּן־לִ֥י בָלָ֛ק מְלֹ֥א בֵית֖וֹ כֶּ֣סֶף וְזָהָ֑ב
לֹ֣א אוּכַ֗ל לַעֲבֹר֙ אֶת־פִּי֙ יְהוָ֣ה אֱלֹהָ֔י
לַעֲשׂ֥וֹת קְטַנָּ֖ה א֥וֹ גְדוֹלָֽה׃
19 וְעַתָּ֗ה שְׁב֨וּ נָ֥א בָזֶ֛ה גַּם־אַתֶּ֖ם הַלָּ֑יְלָה
וְאֵ֣דְעָ֔ה מַה־יֹּסֵ֥ף יְהוָ֖ה דַּבֵּ֥ר עִמִּֽי׃
20 וַיָּבֹ֨א אֱלֹהִ֥ים ׀ אֶל־בִּלְעָם֮ לַיְלָה֒
וַיֹּ֣אמֶר ל֗וֹ
אִם־לִקְרֹ֤א לְךָ֙ בָּ֣אוּ הָאֲנָשִׁ֔ים
ק֖וּם לֵ֣ךְ אִתָּ֑ם
וְאַ֗ךְ אֶת־הַדָּבָ֛ר אֲשֶׁר־אֲדַבֵּ֥ר אֵלֶ֖יךָ אֹת֥וֹ תַעֲשֶֽׂה׃
21 וַיָּ֤קָם בִּלְעָם֙ בַּבֹּ֔קֶר
וַֽיַּחֲבֹ֖שׁ אֶת־אֲתֹנ֑וֹ
וַיֵּ֖לֶךְ עִם־שָׂרֵ֥י מוֹאָֽב׃
22 וַיִּֽחַר־אַ֣ף אֱלֹהִים֮
כִּֽי־הוֹלֵ֣ךְ הוּא֒
וַיִּתְיַצֵּ֞ב מַלְאַ֧ךְ יְהוָ֛ה בַּדֶּ֖רֶךְ לְשָׂטָ֣ן ל֑וֹ
וְהוּא֙ רֹכֵ֣ב עַל־אֲתֹנ֔וֹ וּשְׁנֵ֥י נְעָרָ֖יו עִמּֽוֹ׃
23 וַתֵּ֣רֶא הָאָתוֹן֩ אֶת־מַלְאַ֨ךְ יְהוָ֜ה נִצָּ֣ב בַּדֶּ֗רֶךְ וְחַרְבּ֤וֹ שְׁלוּפָה֙ בְּיָד֔וֹ
וַתֵּ֤ט הָֽאָתוֹן֙ מִן־הַדֶּ֔רֶךְ
וַתֵּ֖לֶךְ בַּשָּׂדֶ֑ה
וַיַּ֤ךְ בִּלְעָם֙ אֶת־הָ֣אָת֔וֹן לְהַטֹּתָ֖הּ הַדָּֽרֶךְ׃
24 וַֽיַּעֲמֹד֙ מַלְאַ֣ךְ יְהוָ֔ה בְּמִשְׁע֖וֹל הַכְּרָמִ֑ים גָּדֵ֥ר מִזֶּ֖ה וְגָדֵ֥ר מִזֶּֽה׃
25 וַתֵּ֨רֶא הָאָת֜וֹן אֶת־מַלְאַ֣ךְ יְהוָ֗ה
וַתִּלָּחֵץ֙ אֶל־הַקִּ֔יר
וַתִּלְחַ֛ץ אֶת־רֶ֥גֶל בִּלְעָ֖ם אֶל־הַקִּ֑יר
וַיֹּ֖סֶף לְהַכֹּתָֽהּ׃
26 וַיּ֥וֹסֶף מַלְאַךְ־יְהוָ֖ה עֲב֑וֹר

Who Is the True Seer Driven by God?

וַיַּעֲמֹד בְּמָקוֹם צָר
אֲשֶׁר אֵין־דֶּרֶךְ לִנְטוֹת יָמִין וּשְׂמֹאול:
27 וַתֵּרֶא הָאָתוֹן אֶת־מַלְאַךְ יְהוָה
וַתִּרְבַּץ תַּחַת בִּלְעָם
וַיִּחַר־אַף בִּלְעָם
וַיַּךְ אֶת־הָאָתוֹן בַּמַּקֵּל:
28 וַיִּפְתַּח יְהוָה אֶת־פִּי הָאָתוֹן
וַתֹּאמֶר לְבִלְעָם
מֶה־עָשִׂיתִי לְךָ
כִּי הִכִּיתַנִי זֶה שָׁלֹשׁ רְגָלִים:
29 וַיֹּאמֶר בִּלְעָם לָאָתוֹן
כִּי הִתְעַלַּלְתְּ בִּי
לוּ יֶשׁ־חֶרֶב בְּיָדִי
כִּי עַתָּה הֲרַגְתִּיךְ:
30 וַתֹּאמֶר הָאָתוֹן אֶל־בִּלְעָם
הֲלוֹא אָנֹכִי אֲתֹנְךָ
אֲשֶׁר־רָכַבְתָּ עָלַי מֵעוֹדְךָ עַד־הַיּוֹם הַזֶּה
הַהַסְכֵּן הִסְכַּנְתִּי לַעֲשׂוֹת לְךָ כֹּה
וַיֹּאמֶר לֹא:
31 וַיְגַל יְהוָה אֶת־עֵינֵי בִלְעָם
וַיַּרְא אֶת־מַלְאַךְ יְהוָה נִצָּב בַּדֶּרֶךְ וְחַרְבּוֹ שְׁלֻפָה בְּיָדוֹ
וַיִּקֹּד וַיִּשְׁתַּחוּ לְאַפָּיו:
32 וַיֹּאמֶר אֵלָיו מַלְאַךְ יְהוָה
עַל־מָה הִכִּיתָ אֶת־אֲתֹנְךָ זֶה שָׁלוֹשׁ רְגָלִים
הִנֵּה אָנֹכִי יָצָאתִי לְשָׂטָן
כִּי־יָרַט הַדֶּרֶךְ לְנֶגְדִּי:
33 וַתִּרְאַנִי הָאָתוֹן וַתֵּט לְפָנַי זֶה שָׁלֹשׁ רְגָלִים
אוּלַי נָטְתָה מִפָּנַי
כִּי עַתָּה גַּם־אֹתְכָה הָרַגְתִּי וְאוֹתָהּ הֶחֱיֵיתִי:
34 וַיֹּאמֶר בִּלְעָם אֶל־מַלְאַךְ יְהוָה
חָטָאתִי כִּי לֹא יָדַעְתִּי כִּי אַתָּה נִצָּב לִקְרָאתִי בַּדָּרֶךְ
וְעַתָּה אִם־רַע בְּעֵינֶיךָ אָשׁוּבָה לִּי:
35 וַיֹּאמֶר מַלְאַךְ יְהוָה אֶל־בִּלְעָם
לֵךְ עִם־הָאֲנָשִׁים
וְאֶפֶס אֶת־הַדָּבָר אֲשֶׁר־אֲדַבֵּר אֵלֶיךָ אֹתוֹ תְדַבֵּר
וַיֵּלֶךְ בִּלְעָם עִם־שָׂרֵי בָלָק:

Analysis of the Balaam Text of Num 22–24

36 וַיִּשְׁמַע בָּלָק כִּי בָא בִלְעָם
וַיֵּצֵא לִקְרָאתוֹ אֶל־עִיר מוֹאָב אֲשֶׁר עַל־גְּבוּל אַרְנֹן אֲשֶׁר בִּקְצֵה הַגְּבוּל:

37 וַיֹּאמֶר בָּלָק אֶל־בִּלְעָם
הֲלֹא שָׁלֹחַ שָׁלַחְתִּי אֵלֶיךָ לִקְרֹא־לָךְ
לָמָּה לֹא־הָלַכְתָּ אֵלָי הַאֻמְנָם לֹא אוּכַל כַּבְּדֶךָ:

38 וַיֹּאמֶר בִּלְעָם אֶל־בָּלָק
הִנֵּה־בָאתִי אֵלֶיךָ
עַתָּה הֲיָכֹל אוּכַל דַּבֵּר מְאוּמָה
הַדָּבָר אֲשֶׁר יָשִׂים אֱלֹהִים בְּפִי אֹתוֹ אֲדַבֵּר:

39 וַיֵּלֶךְ בִּלְעָם עִם־בָּלָק
וַיָּבֹאוּ קִרְיַת חֻצוֹת:

40 וַיִּזְבַּח בָּלָק בָּקָר וָצֹאן
וַיְשַׁלַּח לְבִלְעָם וְלַשָּׂרִים אֲשֶׁר אִתּוֹ:

41 וַיְהִי בַבֹּקֶר
וַיִּקַּח בָּלָק אֶת־בִּלְעָם
וַיַּעֲלֵהוּ בָּמוֹת בָּעַל
וַיַּרְא מִשָּׁם קְצֵה הָעָם:

23:1 וַיֹּאמֶר בִּלְעָם אֶל־בָּלָק
בְּנֵה־לִי בָזֶה שִׁבְעָה מִזְבְּחֹת
וְהָכֵן לִי בָּזֶה שִׁבְעָה פָרִים וְשִׁבְעָה אֵילִים:

2 וַיַּעַשׂ בָּלָק כַּאֲשֶׁר דִּבֶּר בִּלְעָם
וַיַּעַל בָּלָק וּבִלְעָם פָּר וָאַיִל בַּמִּזְבֵּחַ:

3 וַיֹּאמֶר בִּלְעָם לְבָלָק
הִתְיַצֵּב עַל־עֹלָתֶךָ
וְאֵלְכָה
אוּלַי יִקָּרֵה יְהוָה לִקְרָאתִי
וּדְבַר מַה־יַּרְאֵנִי וְהִגַּדְתִּי לָךְ
וַיֵּלֶךְ שֶׁפִי:

4 וַיִּקָּר אֱלֹהִים אֶל־בִּלְעָם
וַיֹּאמֶר אֵלָיו
אֶת־שִׁבְעַת הַמִּזְבְּחֹת עָרַכְתִּי וָאַעַל פָּר וָאַיִל בַּמִּזְבֵּחַ:

5 וַיָּשֶׂם יְהוָה דָּבָר בְּפִי בִלְעָם
וַיֹּאמֶר
שׁוּב אֶל־בָּלָק
וְכֹה תְדַבֵּר:

6 וַיָּשָׁב אֵלָיו

Who Is the True Seer Driven by God?

וְהִנֵּה נִצָּב עַל־עֹלָתוֹ הוּא וְכָל־שָׂרֵי מוֹאָב:

7 וַיִּשָּׂא מְשָׁלוֹ וַיֹּאמַר
מִן־אֲרָם יַנְחֵנִי בָלָק
מֶלֶךְ־מוֹאָב מֵהַרְרֵי־קֶדֶם
לְכָה אָרָה־לִּי יַעֲקֹב
וּלְכָה זֹעֲמָה יִשְׂרָאֵל:

8 מָה אֶקֹּב
לֹא קַבֹּה אֵל
וּמָה אֶזְעֹם
לֹא זָעַם יְהוָה:

9 כִּי־מֵרֹאשׁ צֻרִים אֶרְאֶנּוּ
וּמִגְּבָעוֹת אֲשׁוּרֶנּוּ
הֶן־עָם לְבָדָד יִשְׁכֹּן
וּבַגּוֹיִם לֹא יִתְחַשָּׁב:

10 מִי מָנָה עֲפַר יַעֲקֹב
וּמִסְפָּר אֶת־רֹבַע יִשְׂרָאֵל
תָּמֹת נַפְשִׁי מוֹת יְשָׁרִים
וּתְהִי אַחֲרִיתִי כָּמֹהוּ:

11 וַיֹּאמֶר בָּלָק אֶל־בִּלְעָם
מֶה עָשִׂיתָ לִי
לָקֹב אֹיְבַי לְקַחְתִּיךָ
וְהִנֵּה בֵּרַכְתָּ בָרֵךְ:

12 וַיַּעַן וַיֹּאמַר
הֲלֹא אֵת אֲשֶׁר יָשִׂים יְהוָה בְּפִי אֹתוֹ אֶשְׁמֹר לְדַבֵּר:

13 וַיֹּאמֶר אֵלָיו בָּלָק
לְךָ־נָּא אִתִּי אֶל־מָקוֹם אַחֵר אֲשֶׁר תִּרְאֶנּוּ
מִשָּׁם אֶפֶס קָצֵהוּ תִרְאֶה וְכֻלּוֹ לֹא תִרְאֶה
וְקָבְנוֹ־לִי מִשָּׁם:

14 וַיִּקָּחֵהוּ שְׂדֵה צֹפִים אֶל־רֹאשׁ הַפִּסְגָּה
וַיִּבֶן שִׁבְעָה מִזְבְּחֹת
וַיַּעַל פָּר וָאַיִל בַּמִּזְבֵּחַ:

15 וַיֹּאמֶר אֶל־בָּלָק
הִתְיַצֵּב כֹּה עַל־עֹלָתֶךָ
וְאָנֹכִי אִקָּרֶה כֹּה:

16 וַיִּקָּר יְהוָה אֶל־בִּלְעָם
וַיָּשֶׂם דָּבָר בְּפִיו

Analysis of the Balaam Text of Num 22-24

וַיֹּאמֶר
שׁוּב אֶל־בָּלָק
וְכֹה תְדַבֵּר:
17 וַיָּבֹא אֵלָיו
וְהִנּוֹ נִצָּב עַל־עֹלָתוֹ וְשָׂרֵי מוֹאָב אִתּוֹ
וַיֹּאמֶר לוֹ בָּלָק
מַה־דִּבֶּר יְהוָה:
18 וַיִּשָּׂא מְשָׁלוֹ וַיֹּאמַר
קוּם בָּלָק וּשֲׁמָע
הַאֲזִינָה עָדַי בְּנוֹ צִפֹּר:
19 לֹא אִישׁ אֵל וִיכַזֵּב
וּבֶן־אָדָם וְיִתְנֶחָם
הַהוּא אָמַר וְלֹא יַעֲשֶׂה
וְדִבֶּר וְלֹא יְקִימֶנָּה:
20 הִנֵּה בָרֵךְ לָקָחְתִּי
וּבֵרֵךְ וְלֹא אֲשִׁיבֶנָּה:
21 לֹא־הִבִּיט אָוֶן בְּיַעֲקֹב
וְלֹא־רָאָה עָמָל בְּיִשְׂרָאֵל
יְהוָה אֱלֹהָיו עִמּוֹ
וּתְרוּעַת מֶלֶךְ בּוֹ:
22 אֵל מוֹצִיאָם מִמִּצְרָיִם
כְּתוֹעֲפֹת רְאֵם לוֹ:
23 כִּי לֹא־נַחַשׁ בְּיַעֲקֹב
וְלֹא־קֶסֶם בְּיִשְׂרָאֵל
כָּעֵת יֵאָמֵר לְיַעֲקֹב וּלְיִשְׂרָאֵל
מַה־פָּעַל אֵל:
24 הֶן־עָם כְּלָבִיא יָקוּם
וְכַאֲרִי יִתְנַשָּׂא
לֹא יִשְׁכַּב עַד־יֹאכַל טֶרֶף
וְדַם־חֲלָלִים יִשְׁתֶּה:
25 וַיֹּאמֶר בָּלָק אֶל־בִּלְעָם
גַּם־קֹב לֹא תִקֳּבֶנּוּ
גַּם־בָּרֵךְ לֹא תְבָרֲכֶנּוּ:
26 וַיַּעַן בִּלְעָם וַיֹּאמֶר אֶל־בָּלָק
הֲלֹא דִּבַּרְתִּי אֵלֶיךָ לֵאמֹר
כֹּל אֲשֶׁר־יְדַבֵּר יְהוָה אֹתוֹ אֶעֱשֶׂה:

Who Is the True Seer Driven by God?

27 וַיֹּ֤אמֶר בָּלָק֙ אֶל־בִּלְעָ֔ם
לְכָה־נָּא֙
אֶקָּחֲךָ֖ אֶל־מָק֣וֹם אַחֵ֑ר
אוּלַ֤י יִישַׁר֙ בְּעֵינֵ֣י הָאֱלֹהִ֔ים
וְקַבֹּ֥תוֹ לִ֖י מִשָּֽׁם׃

28 וַיִּקַּ֥ח בָּלָ֖ק אֶת־בִּלְעָ֑ם
רֹ֣אשׁ הַפְּע֔וֹר הַנִּשְׁקָ֖ף עַל־פְּנֵ֥י הַיְשִׁימֹֽן׃

29 וַיֹּ֤אמֶר בִּלְעָם֙ אֶל־בָּלָ֔ק
בְּנֵה־לִ֥י בָזֶ֖ה שִׁבְעָ֣ה מִזְבְּחֹ֑ת
וְהָכֵ֥ן לִי֙ בָּזֶ֔ה שִׁבְעָ֥ה פָרִ֖ים וְשִׁבְעָ֥ה אֵילִֽים׃

30 וַיַּ֣עַשׂ בָּלָ֔ק כַּאֲשֶׁ֖ר אָמַ֣ר בִּלְעָ֑ם
וַיַּ֛עַל פָּ֥ר וָאַ֖יִל בַּמִּזְבֵּֽחַ׃

24:1 וַיַּ֣רְא בִּלְעָ֗ם כִּ֣י ט֞וֹב בְּעֵינֵ֤י יְהוָה֙ לְבָרֵ֣ךְ אֶת־יִשְׂרָאֵ֔ל
וְלֹא־הָלַ֥ךְ כְּפַֽעַם־בְּפַ֖עַם לִקְרַ֣את נְחָשִׁ֑ים
וַיָּ֥שֶׁת אֶל־הַמִּדְבָּ֖ר פָּנָֽיו׃

2 וַיִּשָּׂ֨א בִלְעָ֜ם אֶת־עֵינָ֗יו
וַיַּרְא֙ אֶת־יִשְׂרָאֵ֔ל שֹׁכֵ֖ן לִשְׁבָטָ֑יו
וַתְּהִ֥י עָלָ֖יו ר֥וּחַ אֱלֹהִֽים׃

3 וַיִּשָּׂ֥א מְשָׁל֖וֹ וַיֹּאמַ֑ר
נְאֻ֤ם בִּלְעָם֙ בְּנ֣וֹ בְעֹ֔ר
וּנְאֻ֥ם הַגֶּ֖בֶר שְׁתֻ֥ם הָעָֽיִן׃

4 נְאֻ֕ם שֹׁמֵ֖עַ אִמְרֵי־אֵ֑ל
אֲשֶׁ֨ר מַחֲזֵ֤ה שַׁדַּי֙ יֶֽחֱזֶ֔ה
נֹפֵ֖ל וּגְל֥וּי עֵינָֽיִם׃

5 מַה־טֹּ֥בוּ אֹהָלֶ֖יךָ יַעֲקֹ֑ב
מִשְׁכְּנֹתֶ֖יךָ יִשְׂרָאֵֽל׃

6 כִּנְחָלִ֣ים נִטָּ֔יוּ
כְּגַנֹּ֖ת עֲלֵ֣י נָהָ֑ר
כַּאֲהָלִים֙ נָטַ֣ע יְהוָ֔ה
כַּאֲרָזִ֖ים עֲלֵי־מָֽיִם׃

7 יִזַּל־מַ֙יִם֙ מִדָּ֣לְיָ֔ו
וְזַרְע֖וֹ בְּמַ֣יִם רַבִּ֑ים
וְיָרֹ֤ם מֵֽאֲגַג֙ מַלְכּ֔וֹ
וְתִנַּשֵּׂ֖א מַלְכֻתֽוֹ׃

8 אֵ֚ל מוֹצִיא֣וֹ מִמִּצְרַ֔יִם
כְּתוֹעֲפֹ֥ת רְאֵ֖ם ל֑וֹ

יֹאכַל גּוֹיִם צָרָיו
וְעַצְמֹתֵיהֶם יְגָרֵם
וְחִצָּיו יִמְחָץ:
כָּרַע שָׁכַב כַּאֲרִי וּכְלָבִיא 9
מִי יְקִימֶנּוּ
מְבָרֲכֶיךָ בָרוּךְ וְאֹרְרֶיךָ אָרוּר:
וַיִּחַר־אַף בָּלָק אֶל־בִּלְעָם 10
וַיִּסְפֹּק אֶת־כַּפָּיו
וַיֹּאמֶר בָּלָק אֶל־בִּלְעָם
לָקֹב אֹיְבַי קְרָאתִיךָ
וְהִנֵּה בֵּרַכְתָּ בָרֵךְ זֶה שָׁלֹשׁ פְּעָמִים:
וְעַתָּה בְּרַח־לְךָ אֶל־מְקוֹמֶךָ 11
אָמַרְתִּי כַּבֵּד אֲכַבֶּדְךָ
וְהִנֵּה מְנָעֲךָ יְהוָה מִכָּבוֹד:
וַיֹּאמֶר בִּלְעָם אֶל־בָּלָק 12
הֲלֹא גַּם אֶל־מַלְאָכֶיךָ אֲשֶׁר־שָׁלַחְתָּ אֵלַי דִּבַּרְתִּי לֵאמֹר:
אִם־יִתֶּן־לִי בָלָק מְלֹא בֵיתוֹ כֶּסֶף וְזָהָב 13
לֹא אוּכַל לַעֲבֹר אֶת־פִּי יְהוָה
לַעֲשׂוֹת טוֹבָה אוֹ רָעָה מִלִּבִּי
אֲשֶׁר־יְדַבֵּר יְהוָה אֹתוֹ אֲדַבֵּר:
וְעַתָּה הִנְנִי הוֹלֵךְ לְעַמִּי 14
לְכָה אִיעָצְךָ אֲשֶׁר יַעֲשֶׂה הָעָם הַזֶּה לְעַמְּךָ בְּאַחֲרִית הַיָּמִים:
וַיִּשָּׂא מְשָׁלוֹ וַיֹּאמַר 15
נְאֻם בִּלְעָם בְּנוֹ בְעֹר
וּנְאֻם הַגֶּבֶר שְׁתֻם הָעָיִן:
נְאֻם שֹׁמֵעַ אִמְרֵי־אֵל 16
וְיֹדֵעַ דַּעַת עֶלְיוֹן
מַחֲזֵה שַׁדַּי יֶחֱזֶה
נֹפֵל וּגְלוּי עֵינָיִם:
אֶרְאֶנּוּ וְלֹא עַתָּה 17
אֲשׁוּרֶנּוּ וְלֹא קָרוֹב
דָּרַךְ כּוֹכָב מִיַּעֲקֹב
וְקָם שֵׁבֶט מִיִּשְׂרָאֵל
וּמָחַץ פַּאֲתֵי מוֹאָב
וְקַרְקַר כָּל־בְּנֵי־שֵׁת:
וְהָיָה אֱדוֹם יְרֵשָׁה 18

Who Is the True Seer Driven by God?

   וְהָיָה יְרֵשָׁה שֵׂעִיר אֹיְבָיו
   וְיִשְׂרָאֵל עֹשֶׂה חָיִל:
19   וְיֵרְדְּ מִיַּעֲקֹב
   וְהֶאֱבִיד שָׂרִיד מֵעִיר:
20   וַיַּרְא אֶת־עֲמָלֵק
   וַיִּשָּׂא מְשָׁלוֹ וַיֹּאמַר
   רֵאשִׁית גּוֹיִם עֲמָלֵק
   וְאַחֲרִיתוֹ עֲדֵי אֹבֵד:
21   וַיַּרְא אֶת־הַקֵּינִי
   וַיִּשָּׂא מְשָׁלוֹ וַיֹּאמַר
   אֵיתָן מוֹשָׁבֶךָ
   וְשִׂים בַּסֶּלַע קִנֶּךָ:
22   כִּי אִם־יִהְיֶה לְבָעֵר קָיִן
   עַד־מָה אַשּׁוּר תִּשְׁבֶּךָּ:
23   וַיִּשָּׂא מְשָׁלוֹ וַיֹּאמַר
   אוֹי מִי יִחְיֶה מִשֻּׂמוֹ אֵל:
24   וְצִים מִיַּד כִּתִּים
   וְעִנּוּ אַשּׁוּר וְעִנּוּ־עֵבֶר
   וְגַם־הוּא עֲדֵי אֹבֵד:
25   וַיָּקָם בִּלְעָם
   וַיֵּלֶךְ
   וַיָּשָׁב לִמְקֹמוֹ
   וְגַם־בָּלָק הָלַךְ לְדַרְכּוֹ: פ

The English Text of the Balaam Story by the Episodes with the Textual Footnotes (Num 22:2–24:25)[55]

In my translation, I have emphasized different categories of verbs as well as subjects. Topical verbs are in bold, sub-topical verbs are underlined,

---

55. Walsh, *Style and Structure*, 119. According to Walsh, "The most obvious way in which a narrative is divided into subunits is by a shift in one of the primary constituents of scenic unity: participants, spatial context, or temporal framework. If the shift is prominent it needs no other textual indicators to establish a break. Nevertheless, shifts of place, time, and characters are often accompanied by identifiable textual markers that, simply by being unnecessary, serve to underscore the unit boundary." Agreeing with him, I suggest that the change of episodes is dependent on the combination of the changes of the main characters, the actions of the main characters, and the spatial background.

topically-related verbs are double underlined, and subjects of topical and sub-topical verbs are in bold italics. *Vayhî* is indicated in parentheses.

Episode 1
22:2 And **Balak** the son of Zippor **saw** all that Israel had done to the Amorites.
  3 And Moab was in great dread of the people, because they were many.
     And Moab was overcome with fear of the people of Israel.
  4 And Moab said to the elders of Midian,
      "Now, the horde will lick up all that is around us,
        as the ox licks up the grass of the field."
          And Balak the son of Zippor was king of Moab at that time.
  5 And he sent messengers to Balaam the son of Beor at Pethor,
     which is near the River of the land of the sons of his people, to call him,
     saying, "Behold, a people has come out of Egypt.
     Behold, they covered the face of the earth,
       and they are dwelling opposite me.
  6   Now, please, come and curse this people for me,
       since they are too mighty for me.
     Perhaps I shall be able to defeat them and drive them from the land,
       for I know that he whom you bless is blessed,
          and he whom you curse is cursed."

Episode 2
  7 So the elders of Moab and the elders of Midian departed with the fees for divination in their hand.
    And they came to Balaam
    and they told him Balak's message.
  8 And he said to them,
     "Lodge here tonight,
     and I will bring back word to you,
       as the Lord speaks to me."
    And the officials of Moab stayed with Balaam.
  9 And God came to Balaam
    and he said, "Who are these men with you?"
  10 And Balaam said to God,
     "Balak the son of Zippor, king of Moab, has sent to me,
  11   'Behold, there is a people coming out of Egypt,

Clark divided the Balaam story into three large episodes: Num 22:2–21, 22:22–40, and 22:41–24:25, while I subdivide the Balaam story into nine episodes under three sections (episodes 1–3, episodes 4–6, episodes 7–9) equivalent to Clark's three episodes. Cf. Clark, "Balaam's Ass: Suture or Structure?" 138.

  and they covered the face of the earth.
  Now come, <u>curse</u> them for me.
  Perhaps I shall be able to fight against them and drive them out.'"
12 God said to Balaam,
  "You shall not go with them.
  You shall not <u>curse</u> the people,
   for they <u>are blessed</u>."
13 So Balaam rose in the morning
 and he said to the officials of Balak,
  "Go to your own land,
   for the Lord has refused to let me go with you."
14 And the officials of Moab rose
 and they went to Balak.

Episode 3[56]

 And they said,
  "Balaam refuses to come with us."
15 Then Balak again sent officials, more in number and more honorable than these.
16 And they came to Balaam
 and they said to him,
  "Thus says Balak the son of Zippor:
  'Let nothing hinder you from coming to me,
17   for I will surely do you great honor,
  and whatever you say to me I will do.
  Come, <u>curse</u> this people for me.'"
18 But Balaam answered
 and he said to the servants of Balak,
  "Though Balak were to give me his house full of silver and gold,
  I could not go beyond the command of the Lord my God
   <u>to do</u> less or more.
19 So now, please, stay here tonight, you too,
  and I may know what more the Lord will say to me."
20 And God came to Balaam at night
 and he said to him,
  "If the men have come to call you,
   rise and go with them;
  but only the word which I <u>speak</u> to you shall you <u>do</u>."

---

56. There is a change of location for the background in episode 3, but the episode continues because the change provides a trifle of background information, which is not crucial for the topicality, in the scene.

Analysis of the Balaam Text of Num 22–24

21 And Balaam rose in the morning
and he saddled his donkey
and he went with the officials of Moab.

Episode 4

22 But God's anger was kindled
     because he was going,
  and the angel of the Lord took his stand in the way as an adversary
          against him.
       Now he[57] was riding on the donkey, and his two servants were
          with him.
23 And *the donkey* saw the angel of the Lord standing in the road,
    with his drawn
  sword[58] in his hand.
  And the donkey turned aside out of the road
  and she went into the field.
  And Balaam struck the donkey, to turn her into the road.
24 Then the angel of the Lord stood in a narrow path between the vineyards,
    with a wall on either side.
25 And *the donkey* saw the angel of the Lord,
  and she pressed herself to the wall
  and she pressed Balaam's foot against the wall.
  So he struck her again.
26 Then the angel of the Lord went further
  and he stood in a narrow place,
     where there was no way to turn either to the right or to the left.
27 And *the donkey* saw the angel of the Lord,
  and she lay down under Balaam.
  And Balaam's anger was kindled,
  and he struck the donkey with his staff.
28 Then the Lord opened the mouth of the donkey,
  and she said to Balaam,
     "What have I done to you,
        that you have struck me these three times?"
29 And Balaam said to the donkey,
     "Because you have made a fool of me.
      If there had been a sword[59] in my hand,

---

57. A personal pronoun, "he," is employed unusually in the text.

58. The sword is also the object of the topical verb ראה. Here, the sword is in the hand of the angel of the Lord.

59. The image of the sword as the object of the topical verb ראה continues. Here, the

by now I would have <u>slain</u> you."
30 And the donkey said to Balaam,
"Am I[60] not your donkey,
on which you have ridden all your life long to this day?
Have I ever been accustomed to do so to you?"
and he said, "No."

Episode 5[61]

31 Then ***the Lord*** <u>uncovered</u> the eyes of Balaam,
and ***he* saw** the angel of the Lord standing in the way, with his drawn sword[62] in his hand.
And he bowed down and fell on his face.
32 And the angel of the Lord said to him,
"Why have you struck your donkey these three times?
Behold, I[63] have come out as an adversary
because the way precipitated before me.[64]
33 And ***the donkey* saw** me and turned aside before me these three times.
If she had not turned aside from me,
surely just now I would have <u>slain</u> you and let her live."
34 Then Balaam said to the angel of the Lord,
"I have sinned, for I did not know that you were standing to encounter me in the road.[65]

---

hand of Balaam replaces the hand of the angel of the Lord.

60. A personal pronoun, "I," is employed unusually in the text.

61. I have separated 22:31 from 22:30 to begin a new episode, which is episode 5. Episode 4 (22:22–30) tells about Balaam and the donkey, while episode 5 (22:31–35) is about Balaam and the angel of the Lord. Although there is no change of the locational background, the main characters are differently treated in each episode.

62. The subject of the same continuing object (the sword) of the topical verb, ראה, changes to Balaam from the donkey.

63. A personal pronoun, "I," is employed unusually in the text.

64. BDB, 437. In this lexicon, the meaning of ירט is introduced as the following: (the way) is precipitate ("rushed recklessly in front of me"). Cf. "ירט," *HALOT*, 1:438, where the definition of "ירט" is "to be slippery." Several English versions emphasize the negative nuance of "the way of Balaam is bad" for the word "יָרַט": ESV (perverse), NASB (contrary), and NIV (reckless), while *HALOT* and BDB define the word as "rushed/slippery." According to the definitions of *HALOT* and BDB, the reason that the Lord blocked the path of Balaam in the donkey narrative could be that the way of Balaam seems to be recklessly rushed or slippery in the eyes of the Lord. If this is the case, it is possible to understand that the Lord did not change his mind not so that Balaam could go to Balak, but because he merely meant to prevent Balaam's pace from becoming reckless.

65. When Balaam confesses his sin, he is not referring to his rejection of the initial command of the Lord by going to Balak after all, but not perceiving the angel of the

Analysis of the Balaam Text of Num 22–24

Now therefore, if it is evil in your sight, I will turn back."⁶⁶
35 And the angel of the Lord said to Balaam,
"Go with the men,⁶⁷
but <u>speak</u> only the word that I <u>tell</u> you."⁶⁸
So Balaam went with the officials of Balak.

Episode 6
36 When Balak heard that Balaam had come,
he went out to meet him at the city of Moab, on the border formed by the Arnon,
at the extremity of the border.
37 And Balak said to Balaam,
"Did I not urgently send to you to call you?
Why did you not come to me?
Am I really not able to honor you?"
38 And Balaam said to Balak,
"Behold, I have come to you!
Now am I able to speak anything at all?
The word that God puts in my mouth, that I shall <u>speak</u>."
39 Then Balaam went with Balak,
and they came to Kiriath-chuzoth.
40 And Balak <u>slaughtered</u> oxen and sheep,
and he sent for Balaam and for the officials who were with him.

Episode 7
41 (In the morning)
and Balak took Balaam
and he brought him up to Bamoth-baal,

Lord standing before him to meet him. From this context, readers cannot discover any supporting foundation that the angel of the Lord blocked Balaam's way because Balaam disobeyed the initial command of the Lord to go to Balak, thus acting on his own will. Thus, it is possible to understand that the angel of the Lord does not forbid Balaam to go to Balak.

66. Balaam confirms that the angel of the Lord stopped Balaam because the Lord did not want him to continue that way.

67. It becomes evident that Balaam's way is approved by the angel's saying that he may go. If Balaam's way were not allowed by the Lord, the angel of the Lord should have told Balaam that the way was not good in the eyes of the Lord, and that Balaam should not keep going to Balak.

68. Here, the angel of the Lord actively urges Balaam's going to Balak. These words of the angel of the Lord reveal that Balaam's way to Balak is never forbidden by the will of the Lord.

and **he saw** from there a portion of the people.⁶⁹

23:1 And Balaam said to Balak,
"Build for me here seven altars,
and prepare for me here seven bulls and seven rams."
2 And Balak did as Balaam had spoken.
And Balak and Balaam <u>sacrificed</u> a bull and a ram on each altar.
3 And Balaam said to Balak,
"Stand beside your burnt offering,
and I will go.
Perhaps the Lord will come to meet me,
and whatever **he shows** me I will <u>tell</u> you."
And he went to a bare hill.
4 And God met Balaam.
And he said to him,
"I have arranged the seven altars and I have <u>sacrificed</u> a bull and a ram on each altar."
5 And the Lord put a word in Balaam's mouth
and he said,
"Return to Balak,

---

69. The final subject of the chains of the vayyiqtol verbs, either Balaam or Balak, is not obvious in 22:41. The subject is introduced as "he" or "Balaam" in most English translations, and only Ashley suggests that the subject refers to Balak. Ashley suggests his own translation of Num 22:41, introducing the translation with Balak as the subject of the topical verb (Ashley, *The Book of Numbers*, 463). However, his translation is unacceptable because he insists on a unique translation of the verb וַיַּרְא. The verb is in the Qal form, which should be translated as "he saw (the portion)," but Ashley translates it according to the meaning of the Hiphil form, which is "he showed (him the portion)." Though the only other potion for the subject is Balaam this is also problematic in the sense of the sequence of the vayyiqtol chain. 22:41 consists of three vayyiqtol chains conveying the reporting of the event in chronological order. In the chains, the first subject is Balak, and the second subject logically should be Balak as well, though this is unstated. The third subject of the third vayyiqtol verb that is in the sequential chain, of course, should also be Balak. But, the context of the narrative refers the third subject to Balaam. In this case, it is possible for an unspecified subject not to be the same previous subject in the sequential chains of vayyiqtol verbs. For this feature of verb, I suggest that verb is more topical than noun (subject or character) because Hebrew narrative focuses more on the actions of verb than the subject of verb. This case in the sequential chain of vayyiqtol verbs can be applied to a large narrative unit. If we can treat the relationship of topical verb, sub-topical verb(s) and topically-related verb(s) as a chain of topical verbs, it is possible to find the strong topicality of verb in a whole narrative. Accordingly, in the case of Num 22:41, the narrative introduces the chain of vayyiqtol verbs in which the final verb is the topical verb. In this verse, the actions of the verbs including the topical verb (to see) are more important than the interest in disclosing the subject (who saw it [Balaam or Balak]) of the actions explicitly.

and thus you shall <u>speak</u>."
6 And he returned to him,
 and behold, he was standing beside his burnt offering, he and all the officials of Moab.
7 And he took up his discourse and said,
 "From Aram Balak has brought me, the king of Moab from the mountains of the East:
  'Come, <u>curse</u> Jacob for me,
  and come, denounce Israel!'
8 How can I <u>curse</u>
  whom God has not <u>cursed</u>?
 and how can I denounce
  whom the Lord has not denounced?
9 For from the top of the rocks ***I*** **see** him,
  and from the hills ***I*** <u>**behold**</u> him;
 behold, a people dwells alone,
  and among the nations it does not count itself!
10 Who counted the dust of Jacob
  or numbered the fourth part of Israel?
 Let my soul <u>die</u> the death of the upright,
  and let my end be like his!"
11 And Balak said to Balaam,
 "What have you done to me?
 I took you to <u>curse</u> my enemies,
 but behold, you have actually <u>blessed</u> them."
12 And he answered and said,
 "Must I not take care to <u>speak</u> what the Lord puts in my mouth?"

Episode 8

13 And Balak said to him,
 "Please come with me to another place, from which ***you*** may **see** them.
 From there ***you*** will **see** the extreme end of them and will not **see** all of them.
 Then <u>curse</u> them for me from there."
14 And he took him to the field of Zophim, to the top of Pisgah,
 and he built seven altars
 and he <u>sacrificed</u> a bull and a ram on each altar.
15 And he said to Balak,
 "Stand here beside your burnt offering,
 and I will meet the Lord over there."
16 And the Lord met Balaam

and he put a word in his mouth
and he said,
> "Return to Balak,
> and thus you shall <u>speak</u>."

17 And he came to him,
> and behold, he was standing beside his burnt offering,
> > and the officials of Moab with him.

And Balak said to him,
> "What has the Lord spoken?"

18 And he took up his discourse and said,
> "Rise, Balak, and hear;
> give ear to me, O son of Zippor!

19   God is not man, that he should lie,
> or a son of man, that he should change his mind.
> Has he said, and will he not do it?
> Or has he spoken, and will he not fulfill it?

20   Behold, I received a command to <u>bless</u>:
> and he has <u>blessed</u>, and I won't revoke it.

21   **He** has not <u>observed</u> misfortune in Jacob,
> nor **has** he **seen** trouble in Israel.[70]
> The Lord his God is with him,
> and the shout of a king is among them.

22   God brings them out of Egypt.
> He is for them like the horns of the wild ox.

23   For there is no divination against Jacob,
> and there is no divination against Israel;
> At the proper time it shall be said to Jacob,
> 'and to Israel what God has done!'

24   Behold, a people! As a lioness it rises up,
> and as a lion it lifts itself;
> it will not lie down until it devours the prey,
> and drinks the blood of the slain."

25 And Balak said to Balaam,
> "Do not <u>curse</u> them at all,
> do not <u>bless</u> them at all."

26 But Balaam answered Balak,
> "Did I not tell you, saying,
> 'All that the Lord <u>speaks</u>, that I must <u>do</u>'?"

---

70. In this verse, the speaker of the poetry is Balaam, but the Lord is the subject of the topical verb.

Analysis of the Balaam Text of Num 22–24

Episode 9

27 And Balak said to Balaam,
>"Come now,
>I will take you to another place.
>Perhaps it will please God,
>and you may <u>curse</u> them for me from there."

28 So Balak took Balaam to the top of Peor,
>which <u>looks down</u> the desert.

29 And Balaam said to Balak,
>"Build for me here seven altars
>and prepare for me here seven bulls and seven rams."

30 And Balak did as Balaam had said,
>and he <u>sacrificed</u> a bull and a ram on each altar.

24:1 And **Balaam saw** that it pleased the Lord to bless Israel,
>and he did not go, as at other times, to encounter for omens,
>but he **set** his face toward the wilderness.

2 And **Balaam** lifted up his eyes,
>and **he saw** Israel encamping tribe by tribe.
>And the Spirit of God came upon him,

3 and he took up his discourse and said,
>>"The declaration of Balaam the son of Beor,
>>and the declaration of the man **whose
>>   eye <u>is opened</u>**,[71]

4 >>the declaration of him who hears the words of God,
>>**who sees**[72] the vision of the Almighty,
>>falling down, but having **his eyes** <u>uncovered</u>:

5 >>How good are your tents, O Jacob,
>>your encampments, O Israel!

6 >>Like valleys that stretch afar,
>>like gardens beside a river,
>>like aloes that the Lord has planted,

---

71. BDB, 1060. The verb שתם occurs only in the form of שְׁתֻם which is Qal. Pt. pass. cstr.: "to open."

72. BDB, 302. The definition of the verb חזה is "see as a seer in the ecstatic state." This verb is also used in Isa 1:1 ("The vision of Isaiah the son of Amoz, which he saw concerning Judah and Jerusalem in the days of Uzziah, Jotham, Ahaz, and Hezekiah, kings of Judah") and Ezek 12:27 ("Son of man, behold, they of the house of Israel say, 'The vision that he sees is for many days from now, and he prophesies of times far off'"). From this information, it is possible to infer that Balaam's vision of the Lord can be treated as similar to the actions of the prophets Isaiah and Ezekiel regarding their seeing the vision of the Lord.

7	like cedar trees beside the waters.
	Water shall flow from his buckets,
	and his seed shall be in many waters;
	and his king shall be higher than Agag,
	and his kingdom shall be exalted.
8	God brings him out of Egypt
	He is for him like the horns of the wild ox;
	he will devour the nations, his adversaries,
	and he shall break their bones in pieces
	and he will shatter them with his arrows.
9	He crouched, he lay down like a lion
	and like a lioness; who will rouse him up?
	<u>Blessed</u> are those who <u>bless</u> you,
	and <u>cursed</u> are those who <u>curse</u> you."

10 And Balak's anger was kindled against Balaam,
and he struck his hands together.
And Balak said to Balaam,
   "I called you to <u>curse</u> my enemies,
   and behold, you have persisted to <u>bless</u> them these three times.
11   Therefore now flee to your own place.
   I said, 'I will certainly honor you,'
   but the Lord has held you back from honor."
12 And Balaam said to Balak,
   "Did I not tell your messengers whom you sent to me, saying,
13   'If (Balak) should give me his house full of silver and gold,
   I could not be able to go beyond the command of the Lord,
      to <u>do</u> either good or bad of my own will.
   What the Lord <u>speaks</u>, that will I <u>speak</u>'?
14   And now, behold, I am going to my people.
   Come, I will advise you what this people will do to your people in the
      latter days."
15 And he took up his discourse and said,
   "The declaration of Balaam the son of Beor, and the oracle
      of the man ***whose eye*** <u>is opened</u>,
16   the declaration of him who hears the words of God,
         and knows the knowledge of the Most High,
      ***who* sees** the vision of the Almighty,
         falling down, but having ***his eyes*** <u>uncovered</u>:
17   ***I* see** him, but not now;
   I <u>behold</u> him, but not near:

> a star shall come out of Jacob,
> and a scepter shall rise out of Israel;
> and it shall crush the forehead of Moab
> and it will break down all the sons of Sheth.
18 > And Edom shall be a possession;
> and Seir, his enemies, shall be a possession.
> And Israel is doing valiantly.
19 > And one from Jacob shall exercise dominion
> and it will destroy the remnant from the city!"

20 Then *he* **saw** Amalek
and he took up his discourse and said,
> "Amalek was the first among the nations,
> but its end is utter destruction."

21 And *he* **saw** the Kenite,
and he took up his discourse and said,
> "Strong is your dwelling place,
> and your nest is set in the rock.
22 > Nevertheless, Kain shall be burned;
> how long will Asshur keep you captive?"

23 And he took up his discourse and said,
> "Alas, who shall live when God does this?
24 > But ships shall come from Kittim
> and they shall afflict Asshur and will afflict Eber;
> and he/they also until utter destruction."

25 Then Balaam rose
and he departed
and he returned to his place.
> And Balak also went his way.

The Verbs of the Balaam Story in Num 22–24

Introduction

In this section, I will first analyze the verbal forms in the Balaam text. Based on this analysis, I will discuss the relationship between the verbal forms and the flow of the storyline, and, further, whether the verbal forms influence the revelation of the message and the intention of the story.

Second, I will introduce the topical verb, the sub-topical verbs, and the topically-related verbs in the Balaam story of Num 22–24. It is important to examine the verbs which influence the topical flow of the story. I believe that the structure, the message, and the intention of the Balaam text are revealed through this analysis of the uses of all the topical verbs, sub-topical verbs, and the topically-related verbs.

Analysis of the Verbal Forms in the Balaam Story

THE OCCURRENCES OF THE SPECIFIC VERBAL FORMS IN THE NARRATIVES AND POETIC SECTIONS OF THE BALAAM STORY

Table 1. The Occurrences of the Verbal Forms of the Balaam Story

	Verbal form	Narrative	Poetry
1	Vayyiqtol (134)	134	x
2	V + Perfect (14)	4	10
3	V+ Imperfect (9)	3	6
4	Perfect (59)	44	15
5	Imperfect (75)	47	28
6	Infinitive (46)	43	3
7	Imperative (32)	25	7
8	Participle (24)	14	10
9	Q. Pass. Impf (1)	1	x
10	Q. Pass. Part (8)	3	5

According to this analysis of the verbal forms in the Balaam story in Num 22–24, ten kinds of Hebrew verbal forms appear in the text. Various verbal forms are distributed in both narrative and poetic genres in the text. It is difficult to maintain that specific verbal forms are used in certain genres exclusively with the exception of vayyiqtol and Qal. Pass. Impf. In the case of the verbal form of Q. Pass. Impf, it occurs so rarely in Old Testament texts that the absence of the form in the poetic sections of the Balaam story cannot be treated under a specific rule of use according to genres. On the other hand, the vayyiqtol form is a major form that occurs in the Hebrew narratives of the OT, as well as throughout the whole text of the Balaam story. Interestingly, the vayyiqtol form is used in the narrative portions exclusively. It never appears in the poetic sections. This means that the vayyiqtol is the preferred verbal form of the prosaic narrative.

Analysis of the Balaam Text of Num 22–24

Verses Beginning the Sentence without the Vayyiqtol Verb

Table 2. Verses Beginning the Sentence without the Vayyiqtol Verb

Genre	Verse
Prose (Narrative)	22:41 (V+yehi)
Direct Speech	22:6, 11, 17, 19; 24:11, 13, 14
Poetry	23:8, 9, 10, 19, 20, 21, 22, 23, 24; 24:4, 5, 6, 7, 8, 9, 16, 17, 18, 19, 22, 24

Most direct speech and poetic sections do not prefer the vayyiqtol form to begin the sentence, while the prose parts predominantly use the vayyiqtol form to begin sentence except for 22:41 which manifested the changes of time and place.

All Verbal Forms in the Balaam Story in Detail According to the Genres and the Episodes

(Genres: N [Narrative], DS [Direct Speech] and P [Poetry])

(V: Vayyiqtol, V+P: Vav+Perfect, V+I: Vav+Imperfect, P: Perfect, Imp: Imperfect, Inf: Infinitive, Impr: Imperative, Part: Participle, QPI: Q. Pass. Impf, QPP: Q. Pass. Part)

Table 3. All Verbal Forms in the Balaam Story

Episode	V	V+P	V+I	P	Imp	Inf	Impr	Part	QPI	QPP
1 (N+DS)	5		1	4	4	4	2	2	1	
2 (N+DS)	14	2		2	4	3	4	1		1
3 (N+DS)	11		1	3	9	8	5	1		
4 (N+DS)	22			6		6		3		1
5 (N+DS)	10			8	3	1	1	2		1
6 (N+DS)	8			4	4	6				
7 (N+DS+P)	20	1	2	8	13	4	8	1		
8 (N+DS+P)	15	2	2	8	17	4	7	2		
9 (N+DS+P)	29	9	3	16	21	10	5	12		7

The remarkable finding through this analysis is a) that the verbal forms of vayyiqtol, perfect, and infinitive occur evenly in all episodes, both in

Who Is the True Seer Driven by God?

prosaic and poetic parts, of the Balaam story; and b) that the verbal forms of vav+Perfect, vav+imperfect, imperfect, imperative, and participle appear predominantly in episodes 7, 8, and 9 containing the poetic collections.

Verbal Forms of the Seven Poetry Parts (וַיִּשָּׂא מְשָׁלוֹ וַיֹּאמַר [And He Took up His Discourse and Said]) in the Balaam Story

Table 4. Verbal Forms of the Seven Poetry Parts in the Balaam Story

Poetry	Verse	Perf	Impf	V+Perf	V+Impf	Inf	Impr	Part	Q.Pass.Part
1	23:7b–10	3	8		1		4		
2	23:18b–24	6	8	2	2	1	3	1	
3	24:3b–9	5	6		2			5	3
4	24:15b–19	1	3	6	1			4	1
5	24:20b	x	x	x	x	x	x	x	x
6	24:21b–22		2				1	1	
7	24:23b–24		1	2			1		

The oracle formula that begins with וַיִּשָּׂא מְשָׁלוֹ וַיֹּאמַר appears seven times within the poetic sections in the Balaam story. The seven oracles vary in length, but they mostly use the imperfect verbal form, with the exception of the fifth poetic section of 24:20b, which has no verb in the oracle.

Conclusion

The occurrences of the various verbal forms in the text of the Balaam story do not seem to indicate any specific regulation regarding verbal usage by genre, except for the vayyiqtol form. According to the analysis above, I cannot find any evidence that verbal form controls the main storyline or the foregrounding of the whole story. Thus, it is reasonable to suggest that the task to find the main storyline should not be dependent on a certain verbal form, such as a vayyiqtol form. Further, we do not have to consider the topicality of the Balaam text in Num 22–24 solely under the constraints of an understanding of the vayyiqtol verbal form about which a consensus does not yet exist.

Analysis of the Balaam Text of Num 22–24

The Topical Verb, the Sub-Topical Verbs, and the Topically-Related Verbs

The Topical Verb

A topical verb provides the frame of a given text to control readers' attention to the intended message. Thus, the concept of a topical verb is wide and general rather than narrow and specific in order to inform the whole picture of a text or story. At this point, the topical verb needs the cooperative works of sub-topical verbs or topically-related verbs to develop the topicality for disclosing the obvious message and intention of a text or story.

The topical verb ראה (to see) occurs eighteen times in the Balaam story in Num 22–24, as denoted below.

Table 5. The Occurrence of the Topical Verb ראה (to See) in the Balaam Story

Episode	Verse	The Topical Verb ראה
1	22:2	וַיַּרְא בָּלָק בֶּן־צִפּוֹר אֵת כָּל־אֲשֶׁר־עָשָׂה יִשְׂרָאֵל לָאֱמֹרִי "And Balak the son of Zippor saw all that Israel had done to the Amorites."
2	x	x
3	x	x
4	22:23	וַתֵּרֶא הָאָתוֹן אֶת־מַלְאַךְ יְהוָה "And the donkey saw the angel of the Lord."
	22:25	וַתֵּרֶא הָאָתוֹן אֶת־מַלְאַךְ יְהוָה "And the donkey saw the angel of the Lord."
	22:27	וַתֵּרֶא הָאָתוֹן אֶת־מַלְאַךְ יְהוָה "And the donkey saw the angel of the Lord."
5	22:31	וַיַּרְא אֶת־מַלְאַךְ יְהוָה "and he (Balaam) saw the angel of the Lord"
	22:33	וַתִּרְאַנִי הָאָתוֹן "And the donkey saw me."
6	x	x
7	22:41	וַיַּרְא מִשָּׁם קְצֵה הָעָם "and he saw from there a portion of the people."
	23:3	וּדְבַר מַה־יַּרְאֵנִי וְהִגַּדְתִּי לָךְ "and whatever he shows me I will tell you."
	23:9	כִּי־מֵרֹאשׁ צֻרִים אֶרְאֶנּוּ "For from the top of the rocks I see him (Jacob/Israel),"

8	23:13	לְךָ־[לְכָה]־נָּא אִתִּי אֶל־מָקוֹם אַחֵר אֲשֶׁר תִּרְאֶנּוּ "Please come with me to another place, from which you may see them."
	23:13	מִשָּׁם אֶפֶס קָצֵהוּ תִרְאֶה "From there you will see the extreme end of them"
	23:13	וְכֻלּוֹ לֹא תִרְאֶה "and (you) will not see all of them."
	23:21	וְלֹא־רָאָה עָמָל בְּיִשְׂרָאֵל "nor has he seen trouble in Israel."
9	24:1	וַיַּרְא בִּלְעָם כִּי טוֹב בְּעֵינֵי יְהוָה לְבָרֵךְ אֶת־יִשְׂרָאֵל "And Balaam saw that it pleased the Lord to bless Israel,"
	24:2	וַיַּרְא אֶת־יִשְׂרָאֵל שֹׁכֵן לִשְׁבָטָיו "and he saw Israel encamping tribe by tribe."
	24:17	אֶרְאֶנּוּ וְלֹא עַתָּה "I see him, but not now"
	24:20	וַיַּרְא אֶת־עֲמָלֵק "Then he saw Amalek"
	24:21	וַיַּרְא אֶת־הַקֵּינִי "And he saw the Kenite,"

The verb ראה is the only verb in the heading (Num 22:2) of the Balaam story in Num 22:2–24:2, and is therefore the only candidate for the topical verb. This topical verb, ראה, is widely distributed throughout the whole text except for episodes 2, 3, and 6. The prevailing occurrences of the topical verb ראה show that the two narratives, which are Num 22:2–21 (episodes 1, 2, and 3) and Num 22:22–35 (episodes 4 and 5), and the poetic section, which is Num 22:41–24:25 (episodes 7, 8, and 9), are united around the topicality of the topical verb ראה.[73] Interestingly, the beginning episodes in each major section (1, 4, and 7) contain the topical verb ראה. The major new scenes begin with the topical verb. This pattern shows that the Balaam story maintains topicality through the implementation of ראה.

---

73. Episode 6 (Num 22:36–40) can be treated as an appendix to the narrative of Num 22:22–35, or it could be an independent narrative that is distinctive from the previous narrative. Regardless, I will deal with episode 6 as a minor unit compared to the other two narratives. For the poetic sections of Num 22:41–24:25, the episodes 7, 8, and 9 consist of mixed genres of prose and poetry. However, the poetry is predominant in the concentration of attention and the importance of content and message in these episodes.

Analysis of the Balaam Text of Num 22–24

The Sub-Topical Verbs

The occurrence of sub-topical verb is optional. Some texts employ sub-topical verb, while others do not need it to develop the topicality. In the case of the Balaam story, the sub-topical verbs are synonyms with the topical verb. The synonyms function as various expressions of the topical verb, as helpers of the topical verb for effective revelation of the topicality, or as mediators, if necessary, focusing on a specific nuance of the topical verb, between the topical verb and the topically-related verbs.

In the Balaam story, the reason that the sub-topical verbs appear many times is to bridge the topical verb and the topically-related verbs closely. The bridging function of the sub-topical verb also delivers the specific nuance of the topical verb. Thus, when the first sub-topical verb meets with the topically-related verb for the first time, section 2 has the climax of the Balaam story. This work of the sub-topical verbs helps to make the Balaam story look well-organized.

The sub-topical verbs have a meaning similar to the topical verb. These verbs occur ten times in the Balaam story as listed below.

Table 6. The Occurrence of the Sub-Topical Verbs in the Balaam Story

Episode	Verse	The Sub-Topical Verbs	Meaning
1	x	x	x
2	x	x	x
3	x	x	x
4	x	x	x
5	22:31	גלה: וַיְגַל יְהוָה אֶת־עֵינֵי בִלְעָם "Then the Lord uncovered the eyes of Balaam,"	to uncover (the eyes)
6	x	x	x
7	23:9	שׁור: וּמִגְּבָעוֹת אֲשׁוּרֶנּוּ "and from the hills I behold him"	to behold
8	23:21	נבט: לֹא־הִבִּיט אָוֶן בְּיַעֲקֹב "He has not observed misfortune in Jacob,"	to observe

9	23:28	שֶׁקֶף: רֹאשׁ הַפְּעוֹר הַנִּשְׁקָף עַל־פְּנֵי הַיְשִׁימֹן "the top of Peor, which overlooks the desert"	to look down
	24:3, 15	שתם: וּנְאֻם הַגֶּבֶר שְׁתֻם הָעָיִן "and the oracle of the man whose eye is opened," וּנְאֻם הַגֶּבֶר שְׁתֻם הָעָיִן "and the oracle of the man whose eye is opened,"	(the eyes) to be opened
	24:4, 16	גלה: וּגְלוּי עֵינָיִם "but having his eyes uncovered:" וּגְלוּי עֵינָיִם "but having his eyes uncovered"	to uncover (the eyes)
	24:4, 16	חזה: אֲשֶׁר מַחֲזֵה שַׁדַּי יֶחֱזֶה "who sees the vision of the Almighty," מַחֲזֵה שַׁדַּי יֶחֱזֶה "who sees the vision of the Almighty,"	to see
	24:17	שׁור: אֲשׁוּרֶנּוּ "I behold him,"	to behold

The first sub-topical verb, גלה, is pivotal to keep and develop the topicality of the topical verb, ראה. The sub-topical verb גלה functions as the representative of the subsequent sub-topical verbs. The other synonymous sub-topical verbs are dependent on the first sub-topical verb, גלה, in the context of the story. The subject of גלה is the Lord who controls the topical verb of ראה and makes Balaam see what he is required to see. The most important role of the first sub-topical verb גלה is to serve as the medium between the topical verb, ראה, and the other sub-topical verbs. The first sub-topical verb, גלה, functions as the medium to progress the topicality of ראה. In the story, Balak sees (the topical verb) what all Israel had done to Amorites and brings Balaam to curse her, but the Lord makes Balaam's eyes open (the first sub-topical verb) to show what he intends instead. After the Lord opens Balaam's eyes, Balaam is able to see what he is supposed to see. It is to confirm that Balaam successfully hears God's/Yahweh's words earlier in the episode. Through the transmission of the heavenly vision of the Lord to Balaam, Balaam has a status of "eyes-opened" (the other sub-topical verbs) and the power to have the words of the Lord in his mouth and speak the oracle. God previously spoke a true oracle in 22:12 (focusing on "Israel is blessed") that Balaam accurately hears and conveys and again in 22:20 (focusing on "only do what I tell you") that he accurately hears God speak "at night" without seeing and conveys God's word to Moab. Now, Balaam is able to deliver God's vision as well as his words as a fortified tool of God.

The first sub-topical verb, גלה, is indispensable to maintaining the topicality of the Balaam story. The topical verb is the starting point of the topicality of the Balaam story even though sight is granted to Balak as the subject, but it also needs the support of the sub-topical verbs to maintain, develop, and extend this topicality through the whole story. In addition, the first sub-topical verb, גלה, connects the narrative sections to the poetic sections (the oracles) to maintain topicality in the unified story. The first sub-topical verb, גלה, in 22:31 of episode 5 occurs again in 24:4, sixteen times in episode 9. Thus, the relationship between the topical verb and the sub-topical verbs is not hierarchical but reciprocal in revealing the message and intention of the story.

The Topically-Related Verbs

The wide and general concept of the topical verb needs the topically-related verbs to develop and express the topicality of the text effectively. There are two requirements to be a topically-related verb. First, the verb should be connected to the topical verb conceptually; what/why the characters see (in the case of the Balaam story). In the Balaam story, the object of the topical verb (all that Israel had done to the Amorites [what the Lord did]) in the heading exhibits the specific topically-related verbs: (1) what the Lord is going to do ("speak"); (2) what the Lord had done (and will do) to Israel and other nations ("bless and curse"); (3) what the Lord is about to do ("slay"). Second, the verb should be repeated systematically in a whole text or story.

The Verbs of "Speaking/Doing":
"Speaking/Doing Only the Word That the Lord Tells"

Table 7. The Occurrence of the Topically-Related Verbs
דבר (to Speak), נגד (to Tell), עשׂה (to Do)

Episode	Verse	The Verbs (דבר: to Speak, נגד: to Tell, עשׂה: to Do) and the Clauses
2	22:8	וַהֲשִׁבֹתִי אֶתְכֶם דָּבָר כַּאֲשֶׁר יְדַבֵּר יְהוָה אֵלָי "I will bring back word to you, as the Lord speaks to me."

3	22:18	לֹא אוּכַל לַעֲבֹר אֶת־פִּי יְהוָה אֱלֹהָי לַעֲשׂוֹת קְטַנָּה אוֹ גְדוֹלָה
		"I could not go beyond the command of the Lord my God to do less or more."
	22:20	וְאַךְ אֶת־הַדָּבָר אֲשֶׁר־אֲדַבֵּר אֵלֶיךָ אֹתוֹ תַעֲשֶׂה
		"But only the word which I speak to you shall you do."
5	22:35	וְאֶפֶס אֶת־הַדָּבָר אֲשֶׁר־אֲדַבֵּר אֵלֶיךָ אֹתוֹ תְדַבֵּר
		"But speak only the word that I tell you."
6	22:38	הַדָּבָר אֲשֶׁר יָשִׂים אֱלֹהִים בְּפִי אֹתוֹ אֲדַבֵּר
		"The word that God puts in my mouth, that I shall speak."
7	23:3	וּדְבַר מַה־יַּרְאֵנִי וְהִגַּדְתִּי לָךְ
		"Whatever he (the Lord) shows me I will tell you."
	23:5	שׁוּב אֶל־בָּלָק וְכֹה תְדַבֵּר
		"Return to Balak, and thus you shall speak."
	23:12	הֲלֹא אֵת אֲשֶׁר יָשִׂים יְהוָה בְּפִי אֹתוֹ אֶשְׁמֹר לְדַבֵּר
		"Must I not take care to speak what the Lord puts in my mouth?"
8	23:16	שׁוּב אֶל־בָּלָק וְכֹה תְדַבֵּר
		"Return to Balak, and thus you shall speak."
	23:26	כֹּל אֲשֶׁר־יְדַבֵּר יְהוָה אֹתוֹ אֶעֱשֶׂה
		"All that the Lord speaks, that I must do?"
9	24:13	לֹא אוּכַל לַעֲבֹר אֶת־פִּי יְהוָה לַעֲשׂוֹת טוֹבָה אוֹ רָעָה מִלִּבִּי
		"I could not be able to go beyond the command of the Lord, to do either good or bad of my own will."
		אֲשֶׁר־יְדַבֵּר יְהוָה אֹתוֹ אֲדַבֵּר
		"What the Lord speaks, that will I speak."

The first topically-related verb is "speaking" by the guidance of the Lord. This speaking is the commandment of the Lord to Balaam, who cannot speak motivated by self-interest, but should be controlled by the will of the Lord. This specific kind of speaking is related to the topical verb ראה. "To see" in the Balaam story is also under the control of the Lord. It is the Lord who makes someone see what the Lord is going to do (speak). Balak probably strongly wishes to see something from the Lord, but he does not. On the other hand, Balaam sees what the Lord will do because he allows him to see it. Therefore, "to see" and "to speak" are interrelated in the sense that they are the means of the Lord who reveals his work and plans to his intended audience. Both of the oracles that are given to Balaam about not going, only blessing, and then going but only speaking what the Lord says are preconditioned upon the Lord "speaking" to Balaam (22:8 and 22:19b).

The Verbs of "Blessing and Cursing"

(1) The Verb of "Blessing"

Table 8. The Occurrence of the Topically-Related Verb ברך (to Bless)

Episode	Verse	Verb	The Subject of the Verb
1	22:6	ברך (to bless): (תְּבָרֵךְ מְבֹרָךְ) "for I know that he whom you bless is blessed, and he whom you curse is cursed."	Balak's saying
2	22:12	ברך (to bless): (בָרוּךְ) "You shall not curse the people, for they are blessed."	God's saying
7	23:11	ברך (to bless): (בֵּרַכְתָּ בָרֵךְ) "but behold, you have actually blessed them."	Balak's saying
8	23:20	ברך (to bless): (בָרֵךְ לָקָחְתִּי), (בֵּרֵךְ) "Behold, I received a command to bless: and he has blessed, and I won't revoke it."	Balaam's oracle
	23:25	ברך (to bless): (. . . גַּם־בָּרֵךְ לֹא תְבָרֲכֶנּוּ) "do not bless them at all."	Balak's saying
9	24:9	ברך (to bless): (מְבָרֲכֶיךָ בָרוּךְ) "Blessed are those who bless you,"	Balaam's oracle
	24:10	ברך (to bless): (בֵּרַכְתָּ בָרֵךְ) "and behold, you have persisted to bless them these three times."	Balak's saying

According to 22:12, only God can decide to bless the people of Israel. Balaam recognizes the fact that only God has the power and authority to bless the people of Israel, while Balak believes that Balaam can manipulate God's power to change his will toward the Israelites. Balak is negative regarding God's blessing the people of Israel. Balak clearly believes, as he says in 22:6, that it is Balaam who has the power to bless. This seems consistently to be the mistaken view of Balak throughout; besides, that Balaam was thought to have this power finds support from the Deir 'Allā texts too.

Who Is the True Seer Driven by God?

(2) The Verb of "Cursing"

Table 9. The Occurrence of the Topically-Related
Verbs ארר/קבב (to Curse)[74]

Episode	Verse	Verb	The Subject of the Verb
1	22:6	ארר (to curse): (אָרָה, תָּאֹר יוּאָר) "Now, please, come and curse this people for me," "and he whom you curse is cursed."	Balak's saying
2	22:11	קבב (to curse): (קָבָה) "Now come, curse them for me."	Delivering Balak's words
	22:12	ארר (to curse): (לֹא תָאֹר) "You shall not curse the people,"	God's saying
3	22:17	קבב (to curse): (קָבָה) "Come, curse this people for me."	Delivering Balak's words
7	23:7	ארר (to curse): (אָרָה) "Come, curse Jacob for me,"	Balaam's oracle reporting Balak's hope
	23:8	קבב (to curse): (מָה אֶקֹּב לֹא קַבֹּה אֵל) "How can I curse whom God has not cursed?"	Balaam's oracle
	23:11	קבב (to curse): (לָקֹב) "I took you to curse my enemies,"	Balak's saying
8	23:13	קבב (to curse): (קָבְנוֹ) "Then curse them for me from there."	Balak's saying
	23:25	קבב (to curse): (גַּם־קֹב לֹא תִקֳּבֶנּוּ) "Do not curse them at all,"	Balak's saying
9	23:27	קבב (to curse): (קַבֹּתוֹ) "and you may curse them for me from there."	Balak's saying
	24:9	ארר (to curse): (אֹרְרֶיךָ אָרוּר) "and cursed are those who curse you."	Balaam's oracle
	24:10	קבב (to curse): (לָקֹב) "I called you to curse my enemies,"	Balak's saying

The meaning of "cursing" is expressed by two different but synonymous verbs, ארר and קבב, while only one word occurs for the verb of "blessing" in the Balaam text. ארר seems to be used for the concept of the heavenly curse, cursing from God, or God's will to curse, while קבב occurs in the context of the earthly curse, a curse from man, or man's will to curse. Accordingly, ארר is used in the context of God's speaking and Balaam's oracles to refer to the

---

74. Miller, *A Compact Study of Numbers*, 107. Miller mentions that the uses of the synonyms "ארר/קבב (to curse)" is for variety.

heavenly curse. On the other hand, קבב is employed when Balak requests a curse for the purpose of his earthly avarice. Interestingly, in the case of 22:6, ארר is used in Balak's speech because Balak asks for a heavenly curse in the beginning of the story, and קבב occurs in the context of Balaam's oracle in 23:8 because the curse is related to Balak's unsanctioned desires.

The verbs of blessing/cursing are also topically related to the topical verb ראה. The most important purpose of ראה is conveying Israel's state of being blessed or cursed. Balak saw (ראה) all that Israel had done to the Amorites (what the Lord had done for Israel and to the Amorites). Balak also strongly wished to see that God curse the people of Israel, but he does not get his wish (Balak sees Israel faring well). On the other hand, Balaam is led by God to see (what he wants Balaam to see) Israel's blessing. Therefore, the verbs of blessing/cursing are strongly related to the main issue regarding the topicality of ראה among Balak, Balaam, and God in the whole Balaam story.

The Verb "Slay/Slaughter/Die/Sacrifice"

Table 10. The Occurrence of the Topically-Related Verbs
הרג (to Slay), זבח (to Slaughter), מות (to Die), עלה (to Sacrifice)

Episode	Verse	Verb	The Subject and Object of the Verb
4	22:29	הרג (to slay): (כִּי עַתָּה הֲרַגְתִּיךְ) "by now I would have slain you."	Balaam—the donkey
5	22:33	הרג (to slay): (כִּי עַתָּה גַּם־אֹתְכָה הָרַגְתִּי) "surely just now I would have slain you."	The angel of the Lord—Balaam
6	22:40	זבח (to slaughter): (וַיִּזְבַּח בָּלָק בָּקָר וָצֹאן) "And Balak slaughtered oxen and sheep."	Balak—oxen and sheep
7	23:2	עלה (to sacrifice): (וַיַּעַל בָּלָק וּבִלְעָם פָּר וָאַיִל בַּמִּזְבֵּחַ) "Balak and Balaam sacrificed a bull and a ram on each altar."	Balak and Balaam—a bull and a ram
	23:4	עלה (to sacrifice): (וָאַעַל פָּר וָאַיִל בַּמִּזְבֵּחַ) "I (Balaam) sacrificed a bull and a ram on each altar."	Balaam—a bull and a ram
	23:10	מות (to die): (תָּמֹת נַפְשִׁי מוֹת יְשָׁרִים) "Let my soul die the death of the upright."	Balaam—the death of the upright

8	23:14	עלה (to sacrifice): (וַיַּעַל פָּר וָאַיִל בַּמִּזְבֵּחַ) "He (Balaam) sacrificed a bull and a ram on each altar."	Balaam—a bull and a ram
9	23:30	עלה (to sacrifice): (וַיַּעַל פָּר וָאַיִל בַּמִּזְבֵּחַ) "he sacrificed a bull and a ram on each altar."	Balaam—a bull and a ram

The verbs "slay, slaughter, die, and sacrifice" are topically related to the topical verb. The reason is that the object of the topical verb in episodes 4 and 5 is the angel of the Lord (in table 5), and the object, who is also the subject of the topically-related verb (הרג), takes actions related to the topicality of death consisting of the four verbs of "slay." Balaam saw (ראה) the angel of the Lord standing in the way, with his drawn sword, and the angel of the Lord would have slain (הרג) him in episode 5. This action of the angel of the Lord reflects what the Lord is about to do. Continuously, Balak, as the subject of the verb זבח (slaughter), takes action related to the topicality of the verb in 22:40, episode 6, and again does (עלה, "sacrifice") together with Balaam in 23:2, episode 7. Since then, Balaam, as the subject of the verbs of עלה and מות (die), takes action related to the topicality of the verb in 23:2, 4, 10, 14, 30, episodes 7, 8, and 9. That is, these four verbs can be categorized by the topic of death, which is under the control of the topical verb.[75] The topically-related verbs of death are connected to the topical verb.

In section 2, Balaam sees the angel of the Lord at the risk of his life. Ironically, Balaam escapes death because the donkey sees the angel of the Lord. In the scene, Balaam seems to recognize that he should be ready to risk his life to complete God's blessing Israel instead of cursing ("seeing") in the presence of Balak. Interestingly, the fact that the angel of the Lord was about to slay Balaam has nothing to do with Balaam's wrongdoing in the text.[76] Instead, there seems to be another intention (God needed to use the

---

75. In Exod 13:15, הרג and זבח are used together: "The Lord slew all the firstborn in the land of Egypt, both the firstborn of man and the firstborn of animals. Therefore, I slaughter to the Lord all the males that first open the womb, but all the firstborn of my sons I redeem." The verbal language of death is related to the concept of the salvation and grace of the Lord.

76. BDB, 246–47, 256–57. Usually, הרג is used in situations such as private violence, judgment, judicial killing, or killing beasts, while זבח is applicable to "slaughter for sacrifice" in the Tetrateuch (except Deuteronomy). However, the classification of the usages between the two verbs seems to be indistinct beyond the Tetrateuch. There are passages indicating that זבח was used in the killing of animals for food, not for the purpose of

ANALYSIS OF THE BALAAM TEXT OF NUM 22–24

threat of death to form Balaam into a well-equipped tool of God) through the topicality of death by the verbs.

As mentioned previously, there are close verbal parallels between the Balaam story and the story of Gen 22.

Table 11. The Verbal Parallels between the Balaam Story and the Story of Gen 22

	The Story of Gen 22:1–19	The Balaam Story in Num 22–24
The Topical Verb	לקח (to take)/עלה (to sacrifice)	ראה (to see)
The Topically-Related Verbs	(1) ראה (to see) (2) ברך (to bless)	(1) הרג (to slay)/זבח (to slaughter)/מות (to die)/עלה (to sacrifice) (2) ברך (to bless)

The topical and topically-related verbs in the story of Gen 22:1–19 are the same as in the Balaam story. The verbs in Gen 22:1–19 reveal the topicality of the story that God commands Abraham to slaughter/sacrifice his son, sees what Abraham sees, and blesses him as the result of the test. The topicality through the verbs also discloses the important message that Abraham becomes God's tool for delivering the blessing toward all the nations of the earth through his offspring. The parallel use of the topical and topically-related verbs in the Balaam story implies that the message from the topicality through the verbs ראה, הרג/זבח/מות/עלה, and ברך is identical to that of Gen 22:1–19: Balaam becomes God's tool for delivering the blessing toward Israel. The death topicality in both texts is set in the scene that God intends to slay/sacrifice a man on his side. However, slaying or sacrificing his man does not happen in the setting. Instead, through the death topicality, God confirms the status of the man as a tool of God to complete his mission. The death topicality seems to indicate that God has the final authority over Balaam's mission to Balak and changes Balaam's status into being the tool of God.[77] This gateway through the topicality of death is strongly needed for Balaam's successful delivering of God's will in the presence of Balak, who is against the people of God. The repeated death

---

sacrifice to the Lord: Deut 12:15, 21; 1 Sam 28:24; 1 Kgs 19:21; Ezek 34:3.

77. In order to explain the role of the death theme in this section, I need to introduce a topically similar passage to this text. There is some resemblance between the text of Exod 4:18–26 and section 2 (roughly including episode 3 for the comparison to Exod 4:18–26) in the Balaam text of Num 22–24.

Who Is the True Seer Driven by God?

Exod 4:18–26	Num 22:15–40
Moses asks Jethro if he can go to Egypt (Exod 4:18).	Balaam asks God if he can go to Balak (Num 22:19).
Jethro and the Lord allowed Moses to go (Exod 4:18–19).	God allows Balaam to go (Num 22:20).
Moses rides on a donkey while going with his wife and his sons (Exod 4:20).	Balaam, riding on a donkey, goes with the officials of Moab (Num 22:21).
Moses is expected by Pharaoh to be negative toward the people of God (Exod 4:21).	Balaam is expected by Balak to be negative toward the people of God (Num 22:15–17).
The Lord commands Moses to speak as he tells (Exod 4:21–23).	God commands Balaam to speak as he tells (Num 22:20).
Moses encounters the Lord (Exod 4:24).	Balaam encounters the angel of the Lord (Num 22:31).
The Lord seeks to put Moses to death (Exod 4:24).	The angel of the Lord is about to put Balaam to death (Num 22:32–33).
Moses and his wife, Zipporah, act and confess properly regarding circumcision (Exod 4:25–26)	Balaam acts and confesses properly regarding sin (Num 22:34).
The Lord releases Moses to go ahead (Exod 4:26).	The angel of the Lord releases Balaam to go ahead (Num 22:35).

Brueggemann has difficulty interpreting Exod 4:24–26, which he calls one of "the most enigmatic verses in the entire book of Exodus." For him, "the best we can do is to let the narrative witness to the deep, untamed holiness of God . . . There is no hint that God is testing or measuring Moses, but only that Yahweh operates in inexplicable, undisciplined freedom." He mentions the response of Moses and Zipporah: "After her act, Zipporah issues a verdict, giving Moses yet another identity, very different from the one suggested in 4:16. She asserts that he is a 'bridegroom of blood,' variously with the addition 'to me' (v. 25) and 'by circumcision.' Moses's status is thereby changed, and by this curious act, Moses is made safe from the inscrutable threat of Yahweh." Despite some enigmatic parts in the passage, I suggest that this passage tells about the following: 1) the holiness and freedom of God, 2) the change of Moses' status after his proper response to the Lord, and 3) Moses' safety for the journey to Pharaoh with the confirmation of the strong relationship by circumcision between the Lord and Moses (Brueggemann, "The Book of Exodus," 1:718–19, 720). Stuart correctly notes that "God accepted Zipporah's decisive and pious actions in circumcising her son as an appropriate substitute so that God's chosen, yet reluctant and headstrong, prophet could continue his assignment to lead the Israelites out of bondage," Stuart, *Exodus*, 156.

In summary, the core message through the death theme in Exod 4:18–26 seems to be that God needed to change the status of Moses, who is given the mission to deliver God's words properly as the tool of God to Pharaoh.

The identical patterns between the two passages leads us to conclude that they have the same theme and message. Therefore, it is possible that the theme and message of

Analysis of the Balaam Text of Num 22–24

topicality in sections 2 and 3 reminds readers of Balaam's status as a tool of God.

Another reason that the verbs הרג (to slay)/זבח (to slaughter)/מות (to die)/עלה (to sacrifice) are topically related to the topical verb and other topically-related verbs can be adduced by the fact that there is a pattern among the topical and topically-related verbs in the three poetic parts of section 3. In section 3, episodes 7, 8 and 9, which are three oracles, the verbs appear in the following sequence: (1) Balaam sees (ראה) Israel (22:41 [episode 7] and 24:2 [episode 9]), (2) Balaam (and Balak) sacrifice(s) (עלה) a bull and a ram (23:2 [episode 7], 23:14 [episode 8], and 23:30 [episode 9]), (3) the Lord lets Balaam speak (23:5) (דבר [episode 7] and 23:16 [episode 8]), (4) Balaam speaks ("takes up his discourse and says") what the Lord commands (23:7-10 [episode 7], 23:18-24 [episode 8], and 24:3-9, 15-19, 20-24 [episode 9]), (5) Balaam blesses (ברך) Israel (23:8-10 [episode 7], 23:20-24 [episode 8], and 24:5-9, 17-19 [episode 9]), and (6) Balaam, in the presence of Balak, confirms that he speaks (דבר) as the commandment of the Lord (23:12 [episode 7], 23:26 [episode 8], and 24:12-13 [episode 9]).

All the topical and topically-related verbs occur and make the pattern of the sequence regarding Balaam's carrying out his mission in the three episodes. Especially, the death topicality through "sacrificing" in section 3 is continued from section 2, in which Balaam recognizes that he should be ready to risk his life to complete God's blessing Israel instead of cursing in the presence of Balak. Balaam seems to be reminded of the experience of facing death in section 2 whenever he encounters the repeated sacrifice of section 3 so that he is ready for his life to speak as God commands. This is why the death topicality of "sacrificing" occurs before that the Lord let Balaam speak, and Balaam speaks what the Lord commands in the verbal patterns.

Exod 4:18–26 is applicable to that of Num 22:22–40 and that the theme and message of section 2 (Num 22:22–40) is that God needed to use the threat of death to form Balaam into a well-equipped tool of God.

Who Is the True Seer Driven by God?

The Topical and Sub-Topical Verbs in the Sentences: The Subjects and Objects with the Verbs in Differing Genres (Prose, Poetry, and Direct Speech)

Table 12. The Topical and Sub-Topical Verbs with the Subjects and Objects

Episode	Verse	Genre	Verb	Subject	Object
1	22:2	Prose	ראה (to see), vayyiqtol[78]	Balak	All that Israel had done
2	x	x	x	x	x
3	x	x	x	x	x
4	22:23	Prose	ראה (to see), vayyiqtol	Donkey	The angel of the Lord
	22:25	Prose	ראה (to see), vayyiqtol	Donkey	The angel of the Lord
	22:27	Prose	ראה (to see), vayyiqtol	Donkey	The angel of the Lord
5	22:31	Prose	גלה (to uncover [the eyes]), vayyiqtol	The Lord	The eyes of Balaam
	22:31	Prose	ראה (to see), vayyiqtol	Balaam	The angel of the Lord
	22:33	Direct speech	ראה (to see), vayyiqtol	Donkey	The angel of the Lord
6	x	x	x	x	x
7	22:41	Prose	ראה (to see), vayyiqtol	Balaam	A portion of the people
	23:3	Direct speech	ראה (to show), yiqtol (hiphil)	The Lord	Balaam (IO) Israel (DO)
	23:9	Poetry	ראה (to see), yiqtol	Balaam	Israel
	23:9	Poetry	שור (to behold), yiqtol	Balaam	Israel
8	23:13	Direct speech	ראה (to see), yiqtol	Balaam	Israel
	23:13	Direct speech	ראה (to see), yiqtol	Balaam	The extreme end of Israel
	23:13	Direct speech	ראה (to see), yiqtol	Balaam	All of Israel
	23:21	Poetry	נבט (to observe), qatal	God	Misfortune in Jacob
	23:21	Poetry	ראה (to see), qatal	God	Trouble in Israel

---

78. I specify the form of the verbs in this chart simply because the form clarifies if a specific verb is transitive or intransitive.

9	23:28	Prose	שׁקף (to look down), N. Pt. Abs.	The top of Peor	The desert
	24:1	Prose	ראה (to see), vayyiqtol	Balaam	That it pleased the Lord to bless Israel
	24:2	Prose	ראה (to see), vayyiqtol	Balaam	Israel
	24:3	Poetry	שׁתם ([the eyes] to be opened), Q. Pt. Pass. Cstr.	Balaam's eyes	x
	24:4	Poetry	חזה (to see), yiqtol	Balaam	The vision of the Almighty
	24:4	Poetry	גלה (to uncover [the eyes]), Q. Pt. Pass. Cstr.	Balaam's eyes	x
	24:15	Poetry	שׁתם ([the eyes] to be opened), Q. Pt. Pass. Cstr.	Balaam's eyes	x
	24:16	Poetry	חזה (to see), yiqtol	Balaam	The vision of the Almighty
	24:16	Poetry	גלה (to uncover [the eyes]), Q. Pt. Pass. Cstr.	Balaam's eyes	x
	24:17	Poetry	ראה (to see), yiqtol	Balaam	Israel
	24:17	Poetry	שׁור (to behold), yiqtol	Balaam	Israel
	24:20	Prose	ראה (to see), vayyiqtol	Balaam	Amalek
	24:21	Prose	ראה (to see), vayyiqtol	Balaam	The Kenite

The topical verb ראה appears in all genres of prose, direct speech, and poetry in the Balaam story. The occurrences of the topical verb increase in episodes 8 and 9, which are the final episodes. The distribution of the topical verb and the sub-topical verbs, which are the main sources controlling the topicality of the text, shows how often and systematically they occur to maintain topicality through the whole text. In addition, each subject and object accompanied by these verbs are introduced in the table above to show the main characters. The main character is the subject who is active in each sentence and episode. The main characters are not fixed automatically at the beginning of the story. The main characters that maintain the topicality in the story can vary according to the condition of whether a certain character interacts with the topical verb or the sub-topical verbs. For reference, the characters tied to the topical verb ראה are Balak, the donkey, Balaam, and God.

As the story advances, the subjects and objects around the topical verb ראה vary as below:

Who Is the True Seer Driven by God?

1. Balak saw all that Israel had done to the Amorites.
2. Donkey saw the angel of the Lord (three times).
   (The Lord uncovered the eyes of Balaam.)
3. Balaam saw the angel of the Lord.
4. Donkey saw the angel of the Lord.
5. Balaam saw a portion of the people.
6. Balaam saw Israel (two times).
7. Balaam saw the extreme end of Israel.
8. Balaam saw all of Israel.
9. God (did not) see trouble in Israel.
10. Balaam saw that it pleased the Lord to bless Israel.
11. Balaam saw Israel.
12. Balaam saw Israel.
13. Balaam saw Amalek.
14. Balaam saw the Kenite.

In the beginning of the story, Balak sees Israel's destructive power/potential in relation to other nations (all that Israel had done). Then, the donkey, who is the nearest character to Balaam, sees the Divine (the angel of the Lord). Next, Balaam (and the donkey) sees the Divine. Balaam sees certain things about Israel (a portion, the extreme end and all of Israel). Balaam then sees (confirms) what the Lord sees (that God does not find trouble in Israel and that it pleases the Lord to bless Israel). After that, Balaam again sees Israel. Finally, Balaam sees other nations (Amalek and the Kenite).

The subjects around the topical verb ראה are Balak, the donkey, and Balaam, but God, who is the controller of the topical verb, does not appear among them. Among the subjects, only Balaam can begin to see objects, relating to the topicality from the action of the Lord, after the Lord uncovers the eyes of Balaam.[79] The topical verb ראה develops its topical-

---

79. Although Balak "sees" Israel in relation to its power to destroy the Amorites, Balak's seeing is not treated as in relation to the Lord. According to the information of Num 22:2, Balak yet is not aware of the Lord, but he knows the power of influence of the Lord later through Balaam. What Balak sees in the beginning is contrasted to what Balaam sees later: "fear of Israel (no fear of the Lord)" vs. "the blessing of the Lord toward Israel."

Analysis of the Balaam Text of Num 22–24

ity when it meets with the first sub-topical verb, גלה. Balaam is the first character controlled by the developed topical verb. Interestingly, after the topical verb acquires its advanced status, the overall subject of the topical verb and the sub-topical verb is Balaam. This indicates that Balaam is the main topical character in the whole story. Nevertherless, the character of Balaam is considered the tool of God because the first sub-topical verb, גלה, establishes Balaam's character as the only one given the ability to see by the authority of God.

The name of the Divine is expressed as "the Lord (יהוה)" with the first sub-topical verb, גלה, and "God (אֱלֹהִים)" with another sub-topical verb, נבט, and the topical verb, ראה, in episodes 5 and 8, respectively. "The Lord" is the authority of the topicality of "seeing" in the prose of the climactic episode 5, while "God" is prescribed as the general actor in episode 8. Overall, considering all the scenes in which the Divine appears, the Lord is portrayed as a personal speaker (giving his words to Balaam) and toucher (eyes and mouth), with some exceptions.[80]

Interestingly, though Balak first appears as the subject of the topical verb in the heading, he is not subsequently the subject of the topical verb, after the heading, until the end of the whole story. Balak frequently appears as the subject of the topically-related verbs. This means that Balak is a topical character, but should be treated as a semi-active topical character of the text, even though he appears in the beginning of the story. The first-occurred-topical verb in the heading does not make the related character/subject active topical character/subject automatically. In order to confirm whether the topical character(s) are active, readers need to wait until the topical verb develops and co-works with the topically-related verbs to

---

In the first episode, the Lord does not appear as the subject. It means that the topical verb "seeing" with the character of Balak yet does not develop in the first episode. The topical verb "seeing" in the heading works as the topical frame which shows that this story is about "seeing." Balak, who is the first topical character occurring in the heading, needs to wait until the topicality develops to the climax to be confirmed whether the character is the main topical character such as Balaam. This is why I introduce verb (the topical, sub-topical, and topically-related verbs) as the fundamental element, and, further, consider the combination of verb + noun (character/subject) on the basis of the verbal backbone in my theory. Therefore, the fact that Balak "sees" all that Israel had done to the Amorites is meaningful in the sense of providing the topical framework, not as showing Balak as the most important main topical character, equivalent to God and Balaam.

80. In 22:38, God, not the Lord, is described as the one who puts words in the mouth of Balaam. Exceptions such as this are not necessarily due to differing sources of the text, such as J and E or JE, but from free stylistic expression.

reveal the topicality sufficiently. As mentioned above, Balak is topical in the initial topicality, but he gets out of the topicality as the story goes, because he has nothing to do with the sharing of "seeing" between God and Balaam later. Balak sees only what Israel had done to the Amorites so that he fears Israel and does not see "the vision of the Almighty" which is shared by God and Balaam. Balak, as the subject of the topical verb in the heading and the topically-related verb, is around the topicality, but does not involve in the topicality actively. Accordingly, Balak is classified as the semi-active topical character, while God and Balaam are treated as the active topical characters. However, Balak, who is the first subject of the topical verb, is involved in the topical frame of the story: this story is about "seeing." Although Balak is the semi-active topical character, he, as a topical character, occupies an important position with God and Balaam to reveal the topicality of the story.

Regarding the issue of the topical subject/character, the donkey is a temporary and dependent character playing a dramatic role to disclose the topicality through Balaam and the climax of the story in section 2 because the occurrence of the donkey with the topical verb does not continue after the climax. Although the donkey "sees" and speaks before Balaam does, the donkey does not seem to be an active or semi-active topical character because she is not described as an independent character in the episode. The donkey is portrayed as belonging to Balaam. The donkey confesses her servitude to Balaam in the conversation with Balaam: "Am I not your donkey, on which you have ridden all your life long to this day?" (22:30). The donkey's goal in the journey is to serve Balaam as the means of transportation, not to see what God shows. Nonetheless, the donkey "sees" the angel of the Lord. However, it is Balaam, not the donkey, whom the angel of the Lord interacts with after she sees the angel of the Lord. It seems that the donkey is the dependent character of Balaam. Thus, it is not necessary to consider the donkey's seeing as the occurrence of the topical character and verb antecedent to Balaam's seeing. The climactic episode employs the odd "seeing" of the donkey, which is the transportation/tool of Balaam, to maximize the effect of the climactic scene so that Balaam's status, after seeing the angel of the Lord, can look prominent in the topicality of the story: the analogy between the donkey and Balaam (the donkey's seeing and speaking as the tool of Balaam vs. Balaam's seeing and speaking as the tool of the Lord).

The work of the donkey's "seeing" is also limited to the object of the angel of the Lord and ends in this part. The donkey can see only the angel of the Lord, but cannot see what Balaam can see, "the vision of the Almighty." The occurrence of the donkey as Balaam's transportation and belonging, having special duty in the climax of the story, does not continue after the climactic episode. The donkey neither shares the topicality with Balaam activel, nor appears as the subject of the topically-related verbs in the whole story.

Conclusion

The Balaam story in Num 22–24 has the predominant distribution of the topical verb, the sub-topical verbs, and the topically-related verbs. They are interwoven to develop the topicality of the whole Balaam story. As a result, the Balaam story reveals its main storyline and its intended message effectively. In the next section, I will introduce their work in detail in the episodes.

The Composition of the Balaam Text According to Sections and Episodes: The Topical Verb, Sub-Topical Verbs, Topically-Related Verbs, Topically-Related Main Characters, Topically-Related Repetition and Patterns, and the Main Topic in Each Episode

Introduction

The division of the sections depends on the combination of the break marks shown in the MT and the major scene changes according to the flow of the storyline. There is a remarkable blank space between sections 1 and 2 in the MT, and a prominent scene change employing the words of וַיְהִי בַבֹּקֶר between sections 2 and 3. Above all, the main reason to divide the nine episodes into three sections is related to the purpose and the location of the topical verb ראה: the topical verb is located in the first episode of each section, and the frequency of the occurrences of the topical verb increases as the sections progress.[81] In addition, the division by the distribution of the

---

81. Clark, "Balaam's Ass: Suture or Structure?" 138. Clark also divides the Balaam story in Num 22–24 into three sections. However, his divisional logic, as well as where he begins the Balaam story, is different from mine. For him, "the narrator of Balaam's story presents a series of three sections—two episodes and a longer concluding narrative. The first (Num 22:1–20) sets the scene and establishes the almightiness of God's actions in a straightforward fable. The second (Num 22:21–40) repeats the lesson, reinforcing and extending the impact through a seriocomic beast tale. The last (Num 22:41–24:25)

topical verb matches the division by the break mark and the major scene change introduced above.

The Composition of the Text

Section 1 (22:2–21): Introduction

In this introductory section of the Balaam story in Num 22–24, there are three main characters: Balak, Balaam, and God. Balak reveals his strong will for Balaam's cursing of Israel in order to defeat her. Balaam confesses that he can speak only what God tells him to speak. God does not allow Balaam to curse Israel and proclaims that Israel is blessed. The three episodes in section 1 show the topical identity, which is given by the topical, sub-topical, and topically-related verbs, of each character and the preparational stage for the topical development and climax.

Episode 1: Introduction (22:2–6)

(Location: Moab).

(1) The topical verb: In 22:2, which is the heading of the whole Balaam story, the topical verb ראה occurs to begin disclosing and developing the topicality of the story.

(2) The sub-topical verbs: There is no sub-topical verb in episode 1.

(3) The topically-related key verbs: In 22:6, there are two topically-related key verbs, ברך (to bless) and ארר (to curse). These two verbs are involved in the task of the topical verb in the story; Balak wants to curse Israel so that he can defeat the people of Israel.

(4) The topical character by the topical verbs, sub-topical verbs, and the topically-related verbs: Balak. Balak is the topical character in episode 1 because he is the one who works with the topical verb (Balak sees all that Israel has done to the Amorites). It is obvious that Balak is the topical character not because he is the only and first participant/

---

begins as another joke supporting the lesson but then incrementally soars into a prophetic vision imbued with the awesome might of God ordering history through his chosen people."

character of the story, but because he is related to the topical verb in the heading.[82]

(5) The topically-related repetition: The topical verb appears only once in the heading, but the topically-related key verb ארר is repeated in 22:6. The reason for connecting the verbs of blessing/cursing with the topical verb is that these verbs are the means by which the people groups that Balak and Balaam see will prosper or not.

(6) The topically-related pattern: Balak's fear toward Israel dwelling opposite him arises from Balak having seen Israel defeat the Amorites, which in turn leads him to find a way for a god to curse Israel rather than the status quo of Israel prospering (being blessed). This fearful atmosphere of an overwhelmed Balak in episode 1 is the bridge between the topical verb ראה (to see) and the topically-related key verb ארר (to curse). The topical verb in this introductory episode of section 1 meets one of the topically-related verbs, blessing and cursing, for the first time, and develops the topicality of the story.

(7) The main topics of episode 1:

(a) The topical verb ראה (to see) appears at the beginning of the Balaam story; Balak sees what Israel has done previously and where they are dwelling currently, and calls Balaam to curse Israel.

(b) The language of blessing and cursing begins in the story.

(c) The will and message of the Lord regarding the topicality of "seeing" are not revealed yet.

Episode 2: Body (22:7–14b)

(Location: Pethor 1)

(1) The topical verb: The topical verb is silent in episode 2.

(2) The sub-topical verbs: There is no sub-topical verb in episode 2.

(3) The topically-related key verbs: In the direct speech part of 22:8, Balaam asks the officials of Moab to lodge with him to receive what the Lord speaks to him: דבר (to speak, "I will bring back word to you,

---

82. This is the critical difference between Heimerdinger's logic and mine.

as the Lord speaks to me"). The topically-related key verb, דבר, occurs for the first time in episode 2. In the direct speech portion of 22:11, Balaam recounts Balak's desire to defeat Israel after God curses her: קבב (to curse, "now come, curse them for me"). In the direct speech part of 22:12, God commands Balaam not to curse Israel with two verbs, ארר (to curse, "you shall not curse the people") and ברך (to bless, "for they are blessed").

(4) The topical characters by the topically-related key verbs: God and Balaam. In episode 2, there are no topical characters by the topical and sub-topical verbs. Instead, God and Balaam occur as the topical characters by the topically-related verbs קבב, ברך, and ארר. The combination of the topical verb + character (Balak sees) in the heading for the topicality parallels that of the topically-related verb + character (God said to Balaam, "you shall not curse the people [Israel]"). After seeing what Israel had done to Amorites, Balak finds a god to curse her. The fear of Balak calls for Balaam and God to curse Israel.

(5) The topically-related repetition: The topically-related key verbs קבב and ארר are repeated in 22:11, 12.

(6) The topically-related pattern: In episode 2, Balaam delivers Balak's message to God, but removes the last part of Balak's request in episode 1; "for I know that he whom you bless is blessed, and he whom you curse is cursed." Instead, the omitted part appears in the words of God answering Balaam. Balak treats Balaam as the one who can answer his request, but Balaam reveals himself as a person with godly authority. Then, God answers Balaam regarding what to do (not to curse Israel) with his authority. God's answer in 22:12 consists of two imperatives: לֹא תֵלֵךְ עִמָּהֶם ("you shall not go with them") and לֹא תָאֹר אֶת־הָעָם ("you shall not curse the people"). Between the two, the latter is topical because it contains the topically-related verb. Accordingly, the former is not topical or important in the view of the main storyline. Thus, the fact that God commands Balaam not to go with Balak's officials does not have to be treated seriously as contradictory to the action of God allowing Balaam to go to Balak later.[83]

---

83. There are additional explanations for the issue of God deterring Balaam from going with Balak's officials and then allowing him to go with them later. In the scene in which Balak's officials come to Balaam for the first time that God commands Balaam not to go with Balak's officials, Balaam's job is disclosed. God answered Balaam negatively, as "do not go with them, and do not curse Israel." However, in the scene of a second coming

Analysis of the Balaam Text of Num 22-24

(7) The main topic of episode 2: Balaam asked God about how he has to respond to Balak's request for cursing Israel. God told Balaam not to curse Israel because they are blessed. Then, Balaam refused to go with the officials of Moab.

Episode 3: Conclusion (22:14c–21)

(Location: Pethor 2)

(1) The topical verb: The topical verb is silent in episode 3.

(2) The sub-topical verbs: There is no sub-topical verb in episode 3.

(3) The topically-related key verbs: In 22:17, Balak again asks for Balaam to curse Israel through his officials: קבב (to curse, "Come, curse this people for me"). In 22:18, Balaam demonstrates that he must do as the

---

of Balak's officials, God allowed Balaam to go with them under the condition that "if the men have come to call you." This conditional clause seems to be prominent because it is located at the front in the sentence. That is, God allowed Balaam's going just for the response to the calling of Balak.

It is possible to suggest other reasons why God's sending Balaam to Balak is not problematic. First, regardless of the actions of God in second scene, God already revealed his thoughts through the response to Balaam in first scene. Second, although God allowed Balaam to go, the allowance might not be contradictory to God's mind, if God focused on Balaam's response to Balak's call. That is, for God, there is no difference between that Balaam does not go with them and does not curse Israel, and that Balaam goes with them and does not curse Israel. The most important thing is that God still did not change his mind, preventing Balaam from cursing Israel. The clause, "rise and go with them, but only the word which I speak to you shall you do," is the obvious evidence for God's unchangeable mind. Furthermore, 23:19 in Balaam's second oracle reveals the faithful character of God who does not change his mind; "God is not man, that he should lie, or a son of man, that he should change his mind. Has he said, and will he not do it? Or has he spoken, and will he not fulfill it?" For God, it is better for Balaam to go to Balak because, in the presence of Balak, Balaam certainly can deliver God's will. The donkey episode helps solve the possible contradiction through its implicit message to the effect that Balaam could go so long as he "tread carefully" (which he did not by being impatient with his donkey). So, the donkey's seeing and talking illustrate that it was possible for Balaam to not see and thus not speak the message of the Lord, since he neither saw the angel of the Lord nor spoke on his behalf (which even his donkey did).

In conclusion, God's mind is clearly made up about blessing Israel before these two encounters, so that it does not matter whether or not Balaam goes with Balak's officials. 23:19 supports this. Therefore, two different reactions of God regarding Balaam's going should be understood in the sense of rhetorical expression for the dramatic effect of the plot in the whole story rather than a critical inconsistency of the text.

Lord commands: עשׂה (to do, "I could not go beyond the command of the Lord my God to do less or more"). In 22:20, God commands Balaam to speak what he speaks: דבר (to speak, "But only the word which I speak to you shall you do"). As stated previously, speaking/doing by the commandment of God is topically related to the topical verb because the two actions of speaking/doing and seeing are controlled by the will of God. According to the topical verb and the character, Balak sees Israel prosper and wants to do something about it through cursing. Then, the way of cursing can be possible through speaking it.

(4) The topical characters by the topically-related key verbs: Balak, Balaam, and God. As in episode 2, there are only the topical characters by the topically-related verbs in episode 3. Balak, Balaam, and God occur as the topical characters with the topically-related verbs קבב, דבר, and עשׂה.

(5) The topically-related repetition: The topically-related key phrases with דבר/עשׂה are repeated in 22:18, 20.

(6) The topically-related pattern: As in episode 2, episode 3 does not have the topical and sub-topical verbs. Instead, a new topically-related key verb, דבר/עשׂה, appears. The previous topically-related verb, קבב, and the new one, דבר/עשׂה, work together to strengthen the topical development in episode 3.

(7) The main topic of episode 3: Balak again asks for Balaam to curse Israel. But, Balaam demonstrates that he must do as the Lord commands. God commands Balaam to speak as he commands. Then, God lets Balaam go with the officials of Balak.

Section 2 (22:22–40): Body

In this section, the topical verb begins to reappear and reveals the topical climax. In addition, the unique theme of death, indicated by the topically-related verbs of "slay, slaughter, and die," bolsters the topical climax of the topical verb.[84]

---

84. The topically-related verbs of "blessing and cursing" do not appear in section 2. The death theme of the topically-related verbs of "slay, slaughter, die, and sacrifice" seem to replace them, regardless of the wide-spreading topically-related verb of "speaking" in the whole sections. The topically-related verbs of "blessing/cursing" and "slay/slaughter/die/sacrifice" appear in sections 1 and 2 in turn: section 1 ("blessing/cursing") and section 2 ("slay/slaughter/die/sacrifice"). However, they coexist in section 3 with the

Analysis of the Balaam Text of Num 22–24

Episode 4: Introduction (22:22–30)

(Location: On Balaam's Way to Moab 1)

(1) The topical verb: In the introductory part of the section 2 (body), the topical verb ראה reappears. The topical verb occurs three times in 22:23, 25 and 27.

(2) The sub-topical verbs: There is still no sub-topical verb in episode 4.

(3) The topically-related key verbs: The death theme of the topically-related verbs of הרג (to slay), זבח (to slaughter), מות (to die), and עלה (to sacrifice) predominate in sections 2 and 3. The verb הרג occurs in this episode.

(4) The topical characters by the topical verbs, sub-topical verbs, and topically-related verbs: The donkey and Balaam. The donkey and the angel of the Lord are connected to the topical verb, while Balaam and the donkey are related to the topically-related verb. The donkey sees the angel of the Lord with the sword in his hand. Seeing the angel bewilders the donkey to the point that Balaam almost slays the donkey. These three characters are interconnected by the death theme of the topically-related verb "slay" (sword).

(5) The topically-related repetition: The topical verb ראה is repeated three times in the same events. The exact clauses repeated are "the donkey saw the angel of the Lord" and "Balaam struck the donkey." As mentioned on pages 86–91, the dynamic role of the donkey works to support the topicality of Balaam instead of the donkey.

(6) The topically-related pattern: In the introduction of section 2, the topical verb works with the topically-related verb "slay" and further develops the topicality of the story.

(7) The main topic of episode 4: Balaam departs to Balak's place. Balaam responds to the donkey's thrice repeated actions regarding his going to Balak. The donkey responds to the attitude of Balaam.

---

topically-related verb "speaking."

Who Is the True Seer Driven by God?

Episode 5: Body (22:31–35)

(Location: On Balaam's Way to Moab 2)

(1) The topical verb: The topical verb occurs in 22:31 and 33.

(2) The sub-topical verbs: The sub-topical verb גלה (to uncover [the eyes]) in 22:31.

(3) The topically-related key verbs: The topically-related verbs הרג (to slay) and דבר (to speak) appear in 22:33 and 35.

(4) The topical character by the topical verbs, sub-topical verbs, and the topically-related verbs: the Lord, the angel of the Lord, Balaam (eyes), and the donkey. The Lord uncovers the eyes of Balaam. Balaam sees the angel of the Lord. The angel of the Lord makes Balaam realize that the donkey saw the angel of the Lord. The angel of the Lord nearly slays Balaam. Balaam confesses his current status, his sinful nature, and what he does not see and entrusts what to do to the Lord. The angel of the Lord lets him go with the confirmation that Balaam is ready to do as the Lord commands.

(5) The topically-related repetition: The topically-related repetition doesn't occur in episode 5.

(6) The topically-related pattern: The topical verb takes two subjects, Balaam and the donkey. The work of the sub-topical verb (uncovering Balaam's eyes) makes the topical verb function (Balaam's seeing the angel of the Lord). The following topically-related verbs (הרג [to slay] and דבר [to speak]) are used to show what the topical and sub-topical verbs embody in the ongoing topicality; to uncover Balaam's eyes in order to show Balaam the angel of the Lord, who equips Balaam to speak the words of the Lord at the risk of death.

(7) The main topic of episode 5: In this episode, Balaam is able to see the angel of the Lord because the Lord uncovers the eyes of Balaam (the donkey's ability to see the angel of the Lord is not necessary to be treated as crucial because it seems that the donkey is the dependent character of Balaam). Confronted with death, Balaam confesses his current status, his sinful nature, and what he does not see and entrusts what to do to the Lord. The angel of the Lord equips Balaam for the mission to see what the Lord shows and speak what the Lord puts in his mouth at the risk of his own life. Balaam recognizes that he

is only a tool of the Lord for his mission. The angel of the Lord lets him go with the confirmation that Balaam is ready to do as the Lord commands.

(8) Special features of episode 5: Episode 5 is the climax of the Balaam story in Num 22:2–24:25 because the peak of the topical verb's topicality appears in this episode. The peak of the topicality is made of the contact point between the topical verb and the first sub-topical verb גלה (to uncover [the eyes]). Episode 5 is the place for that phenomenon. Since the heading, the topical verb has maintained the topicality regarding what Balaam and Balak see; Balaam has to see (what God allows) and Balak has seen Israel's triumph which spawns the quest for cursing/blessing. The contact point between the topical verb and the first sub-topical verb shapes the ongoing direction of the topical verb in the story; the Lord opens Balaam's eyes to make him see what God allows.

Episode 6: Conclusion (22:36–40)

(Location: The City Near the Arnon and Kiriath-chuzoth in Moab)

(1) The topical verb: The topical verb does not occur in this episode. This fact does not affect the topical development of the topical verb because the topical verb occurs in all sections regularly.

(2) The sub-topical verbs: The sub-topical verb does not appear in this episode. The occurrence of the sub-topical verb is unnecessary if the topically-related verbs are successful at developing the topicality.

(3) The topically-related key verbs: The topically-related verbs דבר (to speak) and זבח (to slaughter) appear in 22:38 and 40 respectively.

(4) The topical characters by the topical verbs, sub-topical verbs, and topically-related verbs: Balaam and Balak. Balaam proclaims that he shall speak the word that God puts in his mouth. After Balaam's words, Balak slaughters oxen and sheep to serve to Balaam and the officials with him.

(5) The topically-related repetition: There is no topically-related repetition in this episode.

(6) The topically-related pattern: Balak slaughters in episode 6, while Balaam is not slaughtered by the angel of the Lord (nor is the donkey slaughtered by Balaam in episode 4.).

(7) The main topic of episode 6: Balaam arrives at Balak's place. Balaam is asked three questions regarding his deliberate coming to Balak. Balaam responds to Balak resolutely. Balak then slaughters oxen and sheep for Balaam.

Section 3 (22:41–24:25): Conclusion

This section is the conclusion of the Balaam story. The topicality of the story takes a definite form in this section. The results contain the beautifully-written oracles in the form of poetry.

Episode 7: Introduction (22:41–23:12)

(Location: Bamoth-baal)

(1) The topical verb: In the introduction of the final section, the topical verb occurs in 22:41, 23:3, 9. The topical verb appears as the *Hiphil* (יַרְאֵנִי, "he shows me") in 23:3 in the sense of emphasizing that the Lord is the authority permitting access to the contents of "seeing" in the Balaam story. The topical verb in 23:9 is used at the moment that Balaam truly sees Israel, the people of the Lord.

(2) The sub-topical verbs: The sub-topical verb שׁור (to behold) in 23:9 is the first sub-topical verb appearing in the poetic parts of the story. The verb is also used with the topical verb in the scene describing Balaam's seeing Israel.

(3) The topically-related key verbs: The verb ארר (to curse) appears in 23:7. The verb קבב (to curse) appears in 23:8. The verb מות (to die) appears in 23:10. The verb עלה (to sacrifice) appears in 23:2, 4. The verb דבר (to speak) appears in 23:12. In 23:11, two verbs, קבב (to curse) and ברך (to bless), occur.

(4) The topical characters by the topical verbs, sub-topical verbs, and topically-related verbs: Balaam, the Lord (God), and Balak. Balaam sees Israel, and delivers the word of the Lord. Balaam does not curse

but blesses Israel as the Lord shows him the blessed people. Balaam sacrifices a bull and a ram, and adds a comment on his desire for an upright death. Balak complains to Balaam for his blessing of Israel. Balaam confirms that he should speak as the Lord commands.

(5) The topically-related repetition: The language of cursing/blessing is used both in the prosaic and poetic parts.

(6) The topically-related pattern: In the introduction to section 3, the topical verb shows the topical consequences through the cooperative work with the sub-topical verb and the topically-related verbs, as well as continues and develops the topicality in the story.

(7) The main topic of episode 7: Balak asks for Balaam to curse Israel in the presence of Balak. But, Balaam demonstrates that he will only speak as the Lord commands. God commands Balaam to speak to Balak only as he commands. Then, God lets Balaam go and speak to Balak. God shows Balaam what he wants Balaam to see, which is the already-blessed Israel.

(8) Special features of episode 7: Ultimately, the topical verb ראה brings the topically main characters, the Lord, Balaam and Balak, together in this introduction to section 3. The characters are interrelated; the Lord is the one who shows Balaam his will, Balaam is the one who should see what the Lord shows, and Balak is the one who desires to see Israel cursed. The occurrence of the death theme here signifies that this delivering of the Lord's words is the significant meaningful action by the Lord's tool, who only speaks as the Lord commands. This tool of the Lord, Balaam, readies himself to speak the Lord's word, utilizing the theme of death on the way to Balak in episode 5. In the first oracle, Balaam discloses himself as the tool of the Lord by mentioning the death theme again.

Episode 8: Body (23:13–26)

(Location: The Field of Zophim, the Top of Pisgah)

(1) The topical verb: In 23:13, the topical verb occurs three times. This topical verb used in the direct speech of Balak conveys his strong desire to see only what he likes. The topical verb in 23:21 conveys the negative result to Balak's desire.

(2) The sub-topical verbs: In 23:21, the sub-topical verb נבט (to observe) occurs in the poetic section. The sub-topical verb works in concert with the topical verb to disclose the strong will of the Lord to not curse the people of Israel.

(3) The topically-related key verbs: The verb קבב (to curse) appears in 23:13. The verb ברך (to bless) appears in 23:20. In 23:25, the verbs קבב (to curse) and ברך (to bless) appear. The verb דבר (to speak) appears in 23:26. Finally, the verb עלה (to sacrifice) appears in 23:14.

(4) The topical characters by the topical verbs, sub-topical verbs, and topically-related verbs: Balaam, Balak, and God. Balak occurs as the first and the topical character in episode 8, and he asks Balaam to curse Israel. There is tension of the topicality between the two topical characters, Balaam and Balak; Balak strongly wants to see Israel be cursed, while Balaam boldly proclaims the blessing of Israel. Balak depends on Balaam for the topicality of "seeing" in this episode. In verse 25, Balak is not the subject who has access to the topicality, but the subject who shows that he is distanced from the topicality by giving up on his wish to curse Israel. Thus, Balaam is the only character who can access the topicality. This is disclosed by Balaam being the subject of the three topical verbs in 23:13. Balaam is asked to see and curse Israel. However, Balaam sees that God blesses Israel and does not see (observe) trouble (misfortune) in Israel. Balaam hears Balak's grumbling that he should "neither curse nor bless Israel." Then, Balaam again proclaims that he must speak the Lord's words. Interestingly, all the topical characters in episode 8 have Israel as their object.

(5) The topically-related repetition: There is no topical repetition in this episode.

(6) The topically-related pattern: The topical, sub-topical, and topically-related verbs work cooperatively. The topical verb ראה and the topically-related verb קבב occur together in verse 13. The topical verb ראה and the sub-topical verb נבט appear together in verse 21.

(7) The main topic of episode 8: Balaam confirms how he must respond regarding Balak's request for cursing Israel. God instructs Balaam not to curse Israel because Israel is blessed. Then, Balaam refuses to tell Balak anything except what the Lord speaks. The same topic of episode 2 is fortified in episode 8.

Analysis of the Balaam Text of Num 22–24

Episode 9: Conclusion (23:27–24:25)

(Location: The Top of Peor)

(1) The topical verb: The topical verb appears in the narrative section in 24:1, 2, 20, and 21, while it occurs in the poetic section in 24:17.

(2) The sub-topical verbs: In episode 9, there are many sub-topical verbs. The verb שקף (to overlook) appears in 23:28. The verb שתם (to be opened) appears in 24:3, 15. The verbs חזה (to see) and גלה (to uncover) appear in 24:4 and 16. The verb שור (to behold) appears in 24:17.

(3) The topically-related key verbs: The verb קבב (to curse) appears in 23:27. The verb עלה (to sacrifice) appears in 23:30. The verb עשה (to do) and דבר (to speak) appear in 24:13. Finally, the verbs ברך (to bless)/ארר (to curse)/קבב (to curse) appear in 24:9 and 10.

(4) The topical characters by the topical verbs, sub-topical verbs, and topically-related verbs: Balaam and Balak. Balaam is the subject of all topical and sub-topical verbs. Balak is only partially connected to the topically-related verb. Following episode 8, the tension between the two topical characters, Balaam and Balak, is amplified in this final episode. Interestingly, Balak is further distanced from the topicality of "seeing." Balak asks for Balaam to curse Israel again. However, Balaam finally confirms (sees) that the Lord is pleased to bless Israel. Then, Balaam sees Israel encamping. At this moment, Balaam's eyes are opened so that he sees the vision of the Lord. From the vision, Balaam proclaims that the authority regarding the blessing and cursing from the Lord is entrusted to Israel. Balaam repeats to Balak that he only can do (speak) what the Lord commands. Finally, Balaam delivers the words of the Lord toward the other nations. Balaam and Balak leave each other, and the topicality around the two main characters ends.

(5) The topically-related repetition: The clauses of the sub-topical verbs are repeated exactly in 24:3–4 and 24:15–16: "The oracle of Balaam the son of Beor, and the oracle of the man whose eye is opened, the oracle of him who hears the words of God, who sees the vision of the Almighty, falling down, but having his eyes uncovered." These repeated clauses show that Balaam is close to access to the topicality of "seeing."

The clause of אֲשֶׁר־תְּבָרֵךְ מְבֹרָךְ וַאֲשֶׁר תָּאֹר יוּאָר ("he whom you bless is blessed and he whom you curse is cursed") is repeated in 22:6

and 24:9. But, the subject of the former is Balaam, while Israel is the subject of the latter.

(6) The topically-related pattern: Episode 9 contains the largest number of topical, sub-topical, and topically-related verbs. The verbs are interconnected across the narrative and the poetic sections so that they coherently develop topicality in the episode. The frequency distribution of the topical, sub-topical, and topically-related verbs demonstrates the definitive conclusion of the topicality of the Balaam story in Num 22–24.

(7) The main topic of episode 9:

   (a) The topical verb ראה (to see) concludes the Balaam story.

   (b) The language of blessing and cursing concludes in the story.

   (c) The will and message of the Lord regarding the topicality of "seeing" are fully revealed.

Conclusion

The topical and sub-topical verbs work with the topically-related verbs to develop the topicality of the Balaam story in order to elucidate the message and the intention of the text. However, the topical verb does not appear in the scenes where the meetings among the topical main characters (the Lord, Balaam, and Balak) take place: episode 2 (the meeting between the officials of Balak and Balaam and the meeting between God and Balaam), episode 3 (another meeting between the officials of Balak and Balaam and another meeting between God and Balaam), and episode 6 (a meeting between Balak and Balaam). It seems that the topical verb of "seeing" does not need to appear in scenes in which the topical characters directly see each other face to face in order to develop the topicality of the whole story.

   The topically-related key verbs establish each sectional topic as well as form the development of the topicality of the whole Balaam story. Interestingly, the prominent role of the topically-related verbs is to provide inner coherence in each section. The coherence supported by the three episodes in each is connected to the topic of the section. In addition, the inter-relationality of the topically-related verbs organize the overall topic of the story.

1. Section 1 (Introduction, Prose): cursing and blessing 1 (cursing is the dominant topic)/speaking 1

2. Section 2 (Body, Prose): slaying, slaughtering, dying, and sacrificing 1/speaking 2

3. Section 3 (Conclusion, Poetry): cursing and blessing 2 (blessing is the dominant topic)/slaying, slaughtering, dying, and sacrificing 2/speaking 3

The verbs of blessing and cursing predominate both sections 1 and 3. However, the nuances of the verbs are different in each section. In section 1, the atmosphere of cursing is emphasized over that of blessing because Balak wishes to curse Israel so strongly that he urges Balaam to come and curse Israel. The theme of cursing increases in intensity as the three episodes in section 1 progress. In this atmosphere, God simply responds to the request for cursing, "do not curse Israel." On the contrary, in section 3, the atmosphere of blessing is more powerful than that of cursing. Of course, there is the language of cursing even in section 3. But, God allows Balaam to actively proclaim the blessing of Israel even though Balak asks for Balaam to curse Israel in section 3. The voice of blessing increases in volume and peaks as the three episodes progress in section 3. These topically-related verbs of cursing and blessing occur and cohere the primary topic in both the narrative and poetic sections of the Balaam story.

The verbs of slaying, slaughtering, dying, and sacrificing are presented in both sections 2 and 3, though the image of death is more powerful in section 2 because the occurrences of slaying and slaughtering in section 2 are unexpected and threatening to the fate of the main character, Balaam. The topic of the verb "to slaughter" occurs in the last episode of section 2 and continues in the verb "to sacrifice (a bull and a ram)" and in varying expressions ("preparing/offering seven bulls and seven rams") in section 3. This topical continuation is sustained through the verb "to die" in the first episode of section 3. The distribution of the four verbs within the same topical category of death throughout sections 2 and 3 shows that both prose and poetry are bound by the same topically-related verbs. The intense image of death through section 2 makes readers pay attention to the core of the story (section 2) and readies them to hear the message from it.

The verb of speaking is uniquely present in all sections. That is, the verb conveys a message throughout the entire story. However, the verb's voice becomes stronger as the episodes progress until the end of the story.

Who Is the True Seer Driven by God?

According to the result of the composition of the text, the verbs (the topical, sub-topical, and topically-related verbs), verbal patterns, and the topic of each episode have coherence in each section. In addition, this organic interrelationship among them in the sections and throughout the whole text elucidates the interconnection between the narrative and poetic sections through a chiastic structure. I will introduce this in detail in the next part.

The Structures of the Balaam Story

The examinations and analyses of the Balaam text in the previous section are based on the understanding of topicality expressed by the topical, sub-topical, and topically-related verbs. From the outcome of the study, I draw the following structures of the text. These structures will help readers effectively understand the message and intention of the Balaam story in Num 22–24.

The Chiastic Structure of the Balaam Story (Episodes)

A. Episode 1 *(Balak sends messengers to Balaam)*

> Topic: (a) The topical verb ראה (to see) appears at the beginning of the Balaam story; Balak sees Israel (what they have done previously and where they are dwelling currently) and calls upon Balaam to curse Israel.
>
> (a) The language of blessing and cursing begins in the story.
>
> (b) The will and message of the Lord regarding the topicality of "seeing" are not revealed yet.
>
> (c) Balak sees all that Israel had done to the Amorites.

B. Episode 2 *(The messengers go to Balaam: God forbids Balaam to go with them)*

> Topic: (a) Balaam asks God about how he should respond to Balak's request for cursing Israel.
>
> (b) God instructs Balaam not to curse Israel because they are blessed.
>
> (c) Then, Balaam refuses to go with the officials of Moab.

C. Episode 3 *(Other messengers go to Balaam: God allows Balaam to go with them)*

Topic: (a) Balak again asks for Balaam to curse Israel.

(b) Balaam demonstrates that he must do as the Lord commands.

(c) God commands Balaam to speak as he commands.

(d) Then, God lets Balaam go with the officials of Balak.

D. Episode 4 *(Balaam's Donkey and the Angel 1: Blind Balaam and the Talking Donkey)*

Topic: (a) Balaam departs toward Balak's place.

(b) Balaam encounters the donkey's thrice-repeated actions regarding his going to Balak.

(c) The donkey responds to the attitude of Balaam firmly.

(d) Balaam encounters the extreme threat of death in the presence of the angel.

E. Episode 5 *(Balaam's Donkey and the Angel 2: Balaam's Opened Eyes and the Angel)*

Topic: (a) Episode 5 is the climax of the whole Balaam story.

(b) The Lord uncovers Balaam's eyes.

(c) Balaam's status has changed to deliver the vision of the Lord as well as his words.

(d) Balaam becomes equipped as the tool of the Lord.

(e) Balaam is ready to go to Balak.

(f) Three main characters' (The Lord/God, Balaam, and Balak) interests center on the topicality ("seeing").

D'. Episode 6 *(Balaam meets Balak)*

Topic: (a) Balaam arrives at Balak's place.

(b) Balaam encounters Balak's three questions regarding his deliberate coming to Balak.

(c) Balaam responds to the attitude of Balak firmly.

(d) Balak slaughters oxen and sheep for Balaam.

C'. Episode 7 (*Balaam's First Oracle*)

Topic: (a) Balak asks for Balaam to curse Israel in the presence of Balak.

(b) Balaam demonstrates that he will only speak what the Lord shows.

(c) And God commands Balaam to speak to Balak as he commands.

(d) God lets Balaam go and speak to Balak.

(e) God shows Balaam what to see.

(f) Balaam sees Israel as blessed in the first oracle with Balak.

B'. Episode 8 (*Balaam's Second Oracle*)

Topic: (a) Balaam confirms how he has to respond regarding Balak's request for cursing Israel.

(b) God answers Balaam not to curse Israel because Israel is blessed.

(c) Then, Balaam refuses to tell Balak anything except for all that the Lord speaks.

(d) The same topic of episode 2 is fortified in episode 8.

A'. Episode 9 (*Balaam's Third and Final Oracle*)

Topic: (a) The topical verb ראה (to see) ends the Balaam story.

(b) The language of blessing and cursing ends in the story.

(c) The will and message of the Lord regarding the topicality of "seeing" are revealed completely and successfully.

(d) Balaam sees what Israel will do in the future.

The Concentric Symmetry Structure of Episodes with the Issue of "Curse/Bless": Episodes 1, 2, 3, 7, 8, and 9

In the chiastic structure of the text, the introductory section 1 and the ending section 3 form the points of symmetry episode by episode on the topic of the "cursing and blessing."

A. Episode 1 (incorrect knowledge of blessing and cursing by Balak in *narrative*)

B. Episode 2 (God's decision not to curse Israel, but to bless it in *narrative*)

Analysis of the Balaam Text of Num 22–24

C. Episode 3 (Balak's strong request for cursing Israel vs. Balaam's trying to confirm it with God in *narrative*)

C'. Episode 7 (Balak's strong request for cursing Israel vs. Balaam's delivering God's firm decision not to curse Israel in *oracle*)

B'. Episode 8 (God's confirmation on the decision in *oracle*)

A'. Episode 9 (providing correct understanding of blessing and cursing by God in *oracle*)

Table 13. The Concentric Symmetry Structure of Episodes 1 and 9

(E. 1)	(E. 9)
"Now, please, come and curse this people for me, since they are too mighty for me." "Perhaps I shall be able to defeat them and drive them from the land, for I know that he whom you bless is blessed, and he whom you curse is cursed" (Balaam)(22:6).	"Come now, I will take you to another place." "Perhaps it will please God, and you may curse them for me from there." (23:27) "And (Balaam) saw that it pleased the Lord to bless Israel" (24:1). "Blessed are those who bless you, and cursed are those who curse you" (Israel). "I called you to curse my enemies, and behold, you have persisted to bless them these three times" (24:9, 10).

The concentric symmetry of A and A': the phrase of "blessed is/are . . . cursed is/are . . ." is repeated in both A and A'. However, the detailed focus is different one from the other; the subject of blessing/cursing is Balaam in A, while the object of blessing/cursing is Israel, who is also mediator of blessing/cursing. A is Balak's words that reflect incorrect knowledge of blessing/cursing, while A' announces the correct understanding of blessing/cursing from God through the oracle.

Table 14. The Concentric Symmetry Structure of Episodes 2 and 8

(E. 2)	(E. 8)
"Now come, curse them for me. . . ." You shall not go with them . . ." "You shall not curse the people, for they are blessed" (God) (22:11, 12).	"Then curse them for me from there" (23:13). "Behold, I received a command to bless: and he has blessed, and I won't revoke it" (Balaam) (23:20). "Do not curse them at all, do not bless them at all" (23:25).

The concentric symmetry of B and B': God's decision not to curse Israel, but to bless it, is announced to Balaam by God in B. B is confirmed in the oracle of B': God's decision to bless Israel is his command, and Balaam cannot revoke it.

Table 15. The Concentric Symmetry Structure of Episodes 3 and 7

(E. 3)	(E. 7)
"Come, curse this people for me" (22:17).	"Come, curse Jacob for me, and come, denounce Israel!"
"I may know what more the Lord will say to me" (22:19).	"How can I curse whom God has not cursed? and how can I denounce whom the Lord has not denounced?" (23:7, 8).
	"I took you to curse my enemies, but behold, you have actually blessed them" (23:11).

The phrase "come, curse this people (Jacob and Israel)" occurs both in C and C'. In C, Balaam tries to receive God's words once again to confirm God's decision regarding the blessing/cursing of Israel. In C', Balaam mentions the relating issue of C; the Lord tells Balaam that he should not curse those whom God has not cursed, nor should he denounce those whom the Lord has not denounced.

In the concentric symmetry structure focused on "cursing/blessing," interestingly, a chiastic relation can be found between the beginning and ending of the story in that Balak sees Israel prospering in the beginning, and towards the end Balaam sees Israel even prospering in the future while other people-groups are doomed to meet the same fate as what Balak saw at the beginning defeat (initially of Amorites, but in the end of all sorts of other people groups).

Analysis of the Balaam Text of Num 22–24

The Diagram in the Balaam Story on the Aspect of the Tensional Relationship among the Main Topical Characters, Balaam, Balak, and the Lord

Diagram 1. The Tensional Relationship among the Main Characters

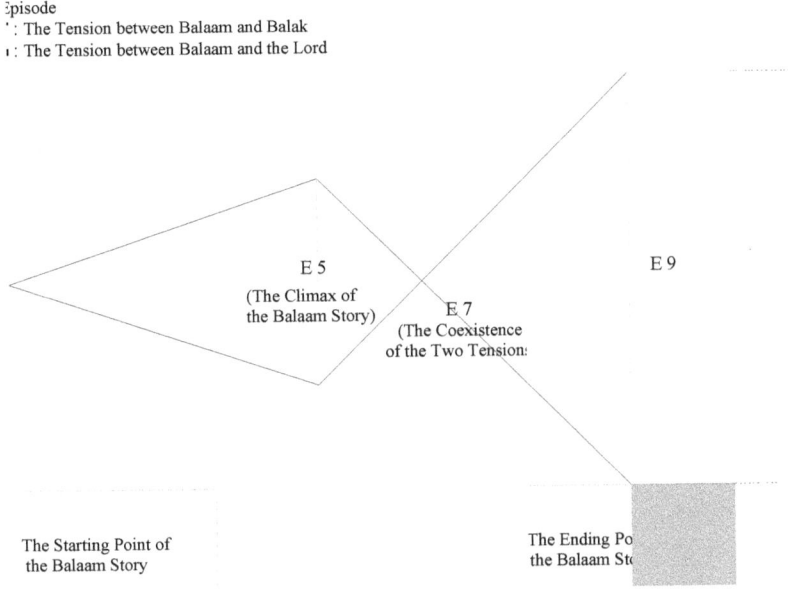

Episode
˙ : The Tension between Balaam and Balak
ı : The Tension between Balaam and the Lord

E 5
(The Climax of
the Balaam Story)

E 7
(The Coexistence
of the Two Tensions)

E 9

The Starting Point of
the Balaam Story

The Ending Point
the Balaam Story

Episode 5 is the climax of the Balaam story in Num 22–24 because the tension regarding whether Balaam should go or not among the main topical characters, Balaam, Balak, and the Lord, is disentangled in the episode. In this episode, the Lord uncovers the eyes of Balaam and meets with him to confirm his message and purpose for sending him to Balak. The most important issue is whether Balaam will speak what the Lord commands in the presence of Balak, since both the Lord and Balak are also invested in the delivering of and hearing of the words of the Lord. Regarding this issue, both the Lord and Balak have already fixed their own positions at the beginning of the story; the Lord must reveal a message of blessing toward Israel, and Balak desires to hear a message of cursing toward Israel. Balaam, on the other hand, does not insist on following his own will for this issue, but demonstrates an open-hearted attitude toward and dependence on the word of the Lord. Based on Balaam's openness for the cursing and blessing Israel, Balaam's choice determines what kind of pronouncement will be made for Israel. As a result, the Lord successfully confirms that Balaam will speak what he puts in his mouth by threatening death, and Balaam

Who Is the True Seer Driven by God?

accepts his role as the tool of the Lord in episode 5. Finally, the possibility for Balaam's speaking arbitrarily on the fate of Israel is interrupted on Balaam's way to Balak in episode 5. Instead, Balaam's status changes to that of a faithful messenger of the Lord. This is why episode 5 should be treated as the climax of the entire story.

In detail, the diagram shows two tensions that coexist regarding whether Balaam should go to Balak or not: tension between Balaam and the Lord and tension between Balaam and Balak. Around the climactic fifth episode, the tensions among the topical characters increase and decrease from the beginning of episode 1 to episode 4. After that, the topical problem of Balaam's faithfulness to the Lord is solved properly in the climactic episode 5, and the first tension between Balaam and the Lord decreases from episode 6 to the end of episode 9. The tension disappears completely as the story ends. On the other hand, the second tension between Balaam and Balak decreases as the episodes progress from episode 1 to 4 with the expectation of their meeting, and increases after the climax of episode 5 in which Balaam and Balak meet each other because their conflict worsens to the end. Finally, the worst tension makes them leave each other.

Interestingly, the phase consisting of episodes 6 to 9, following the climax of episode 5, is opposed to the previous one composed of episodes 1 to 4. As the tension between Balaam and the Lord is gradually resolved, the confidence each character has in each other grows parallel to the growth of the consistency and strength of the message in the oracles of episodes 6 to 9. However, the tension between Balaam and Balak worsens as the episodes progress in episodes 6 to 9.

As a result, centering around episode 5, the relationship and tension between Balaam and the Lord worsens as the climax approaches, then it improves and is resolved at the end. At the same time, the relation and tension between Balaam and Balak improves as the story approaches the climax, then worsens until the final episode when they go their separate ways. My diagram above elucidates that the tension 1 (between Balaam and the Lord) and the tension 2 (between Balaam and Balak) take place and interact based on the topicality by the verbs (the topical, sub-topical, and topically-related verbs). In the viewpoint of the topicality, there are meaningful episodes: episodes 1, 5, 7, and 9. The topicality begins and ends in episodes 1 and 9. The topicality reaches to the climax of episode 5, in which the message and intention of the story are revealed. The topicality is focused in episode 7 (beginning with a "vayhi," indicating that there is something special in this episode: וַיְהִי בַבֹּקֶר ["now, in the morning"]) in which all main topical characters occur, the topical verb and all topically-related verbs appear, and the two tensions coexist.

Conclusion

In this section, I have analyzed the text of the Balaam story in Num 22–24 by examining the Hebrew and English texts focusing on the verbs (the topical verb, the sub-topical verbs, and the topically-related key verbs) of the three sections and nine episodes. Based on this analysis, I have identified the main topical characters, the topical patterns, and the main topics in each episode and section, and, further, the structure of the whole Balaam story. Through my examination, I have concluded that the flow of the story and the message and intention of the text are controlled by the systematic interrelationship of the topical, sub-topical, and topically-related key verbs so that a well-organized structure and delivery of the topicality of the story are conveyed clearly.

In the next chapter, I will introduce the conclusion of this study by dealing with textual issues raised in the introductory part of this study and the theological implications arising from the outcome of this chapter.

Chapter 3

Synthetic Propositions and the Message, Intention, and Theological Implications of the Balaam Story

Introduction

IN CHAPTER 2, I introduced my analysis of the text of the Balaam story in Num 22–24. Through text linguistic and literary analysis, I also introduced how well it is organized as a united and consistent story. The well-organized and consistent character of the text is indispensable to the primary tasks raised in the introduction of this study: (1) to determine the role of Balaam, (2) to demonstrate the unity between Num 22:2–21 and 22:22–40, (3) to show topical congruency between the prose section and the poetic collection; and finally (4) to illustrate the theological implications of the purpose of the Balaam story in Num 22–24. Considering these, in chapter 3, I will synthesize and interpret the data I collected in chapter 2. The conclusion of chapter 3 will suggest the message, intention, and theological implications of the Balaam story in Num 22–24.

Synthetic Propositions

In this section, I will elucidate the synthetic propositions from the conclusions of the analysis of the Balaam text in chapter 2 and reflect on the main questions raised in the introduction of this study.

Implications of the Balaam Story

The Role of Balaam in the Balaam Story of Num 22–24: Balaam as a Mere Tool for Delivering God's Message

As I introduced in chapter 1, it has not been uncommon for scholars to positively or negatively evaluate the character of Balaam based on an incomplete analysis of the text of Num 22–24.

Beyond many passages in both the Old and New Testament, and various extrabiblical traditions that are mostly negative toward the character of Balaam, there are verses within the text of Num 22–24 that allude to Balaam's character. In 22:18, Balaam's words ("Though Balak were to give me his house full of silver and gold, I could not go beyond the command of the Lord my God to do less or more") show that he is a principled person for his work. On the other hand, Balaam's words in 22:19 ("I may know what more the Lord will say to me") are typically given undue weight in forming an unflattering view on his character, such as being selfishly motivated and attempting to manipulate God for personal profit. However, a view based upon 22:19 alone is not acceptable because the previous verse, 22:18, demonstrates that Balaam firmly responded to Balak's officials who requested Balaam to please Balak by going beyond the command of the Lord. Thus, Balaam's words in 22:19 should be interpreted according to the careful affirmation of Balaam in 22:18 rather than an expression of selfish motive.

The contents of 22:18 and 19 cannot be the foundation for a negative evaluation of Balaam's character. Instead, verse 18 belongs to the topical axis that runs through the topically-related verbs (דבר/עשׂה) and is not an independent expression of the character of Balaam. Thus, 22:18 and 19 should be understood in the sense of the topical flow with the chains of the topical, sub-topical, and topically-related verbs throughout the Balaam story in Num 22–24. According to our understanding of topicality, Balaam's words in 22:18 and 19 disclose the fact that Balaam is under the control of God as his tool and do not allude to the character of Balaam. Balaam's role as a tool of God is illuminated by the cooperation of the topical, the sub-topical, and the topically-related verbs in the whole Balaam story.

The fact that the intended purpose of the Balaam story is not to disclose Balaam's personal character but to introduce Balaam's role as a tool of God does not mean that scholarly discussion of Balaam's character is not worthwhile. It is possible to argue whether Balaam is good or evil, but it does not seem to be the primary concern of the Balaam story. My examination of the text in the body of this study through topical verbs does not find any supporting evidence for the assumption that the Balaam story in Num 22–24 speaks significantly about Balaam's character. At best, the conclusion regarding the role of Balaam in the Balaam story should be that Balaam as a tool of God becomes equipped to deliver the will and message of God and completes the mission in the presence of Balak.

The wide distribution of the phrase "I should speak/do what the Lord/God commands" via the topical and topically-related verb (דבר/עשׂה) in episodes 3 (22:18, 20), 5 (22:35), 6 (22:38), 7 (23:12), 8 (23:26), and 9 (24:13), is the primary supporting evidence that the Balaam story is primarily focused on Balaam's role as a tool of God for his mission rather than on the character of Balaam. Through the entire text, the role of Balaam is illuminated by the topical verb and the topically-related verb (דבר/עשׂה). Balaam is responsible for the command of God until the end of the story. In the oracles of section 3, Balaam firmly repeats to Balak that he will speak only what God commands. Balaam finally completes his role as God's tool with this attitude. Thus, using intratextual evidence, Balaam's effective carrying out of his responsibility before God leads to a positive evaluation of his character.

The Relationship between Section 1 (Num 22:2–21) and Section 2 (22:22–40): The Unity between the Two Narratives

In this section, I will discuss the relationship between section 1 (Num 22:2–21) and section 2 (Num 22:22–40) of the Balaam narrative. Most scholars examining the Balaam story in Num 22–24 divide the narrative parts into two independent units, such as 22:(1)2–21 and 22:22–35.[1] According to them, the connection between the two narratives lacks to the point that they conclude that different sources came together to be interpolated in a large unit. However, I will demonstrate the topical congruence between 22:2–21 in section 1 (episodes 1, 2, and 3 in the textual analysis of this study) and 22:22–40 in section 2 (episodes 4, 5, and 6).[2]

First, the consistent attitude of God and Balaam regarding what to show and what to deliver does not support the supposition that God both changed his mind and treated Balaam incongruently in the two separate

---

1. Levine, *Numbers 21–36*, 137–9; Jacob Milgrom, *Numbers*, 468–9; Rolf P. Knierim and George W. Coats, *Numbers*, 260; Timothy Ashley, *The Book of Numbers*, 435, 454.

2. I prefer to the terminology of "section" instead of "narrative" in this discussion because I am not suggesting that there are two separate narratives in the Balaam story in Num 22–24.

Implications of the Balaam Story

narratives of 22:2–21 and 22:22–40.³ In the second oracle of Balaam, the character of God is proclaimed by Balaam: "God is not man, that he should lie, or a son of man, that he should change his mind" (Num 23:19). In the narrative of sections 1 and 2, Balaam also shows his consistent obedience toward God's commandment. Further, Balaam proclaims that he will not change his attitude toward the word of God in the second oracle: "Behold, I received a command to bless and he has blessed, and I will not revoke it" (Num 23:20). Thus, the Balaam story claims that neither he nor God changes his mind. Num 23:19, taken together with chapter 22, prohibits the reader from a facile implication that God has changed his mind.

The works of the topical and topically-related verbs also support that Num 22:2–21 and 22:22–40 are not separate texts, but united and coherent. The topical congruence between section 1 (22:2–21) and section 2 (22:22–40) can be proved by the occurrence and distribution of the same topical and topically-related verbs in both sections. In episodes 1, 2, and 3, the topical verb ראה occurs only in the heading, and does not appear in episodes 2 and 3. However, the topical verb is connected to the topically-related verbs דבר/עשׂה (speaking/doing) in both sections, and to the topically-related verbs ברך/ארר/קבב (blessing/cursing/cursing) and הרג/זבח/מות/עלה (slaying/slaughtering/dying/sacrificing) in sections 1, 2, and 3 to develop the topicality of the story.

The topical development of section 1 can be outlined as follows:

1. Balak sees Israel and calls Balaam to curse Israel.

2. Balaam asks God about how he should respond to Balak's request for cursing Israel.

3. God instructs Balaam not to go and not to curse Israel because they are blessed.

4. Then, Balaam refuses to go with the officials of Moab.

5. Balak again asks for Balaam to curse Israel.

6. Balaam demonstrates that he must do as the Lord commands.

7. God commands Balaam to go and speak as he commands.

8. Then, God lets Balaam go with the officials of Balak.

---

3. The typical source-critical division between 22:2–21 and 22:22 does not alleviate the problem it is supposed to solve because the same "contradiction" that is used invoke the division occurs within both sections, namely "don't go and go" in 22:12 and 22:20 and "go and don't go" in 22:22 and 22:35.

Who Is the True Seer Driven by God?

From the chain of the topical verb and topically-related verbs in section 1 ("seeing"—"cursing/blessing"—"doing/speaking [as the Lord commands]") it can be argued that the narrative of Num 22:2–21 is coherently centered on the verbs delivering the topicality. Accordingly, the topic of section 1 is that Balak, after seeing Israel, requests Balaam to curse Israel, but Balaam demonstrates that he will speak only as God commands (blessing Israel).

The developed topicality of section 2 is as follows:

1. Balaam departs toward Balak's place (The donkey sees the angel of the Lord; Balaam encounters the donkey's three repeated actions resulting from his going to Balak; the donkey responds to the attitude of Balaam firmly).

2. Balaam encounters the extreme threat of death in the presence of the angel.

3. The Lord uncovers Balaam's eyes (Balaam sees the angel of the Lord; Balaam's status has changed).

4. Balaam becomes equipped as the tool of the Lord (Balaam is confirmed to speak only the word that the Lord tells him; Balaam is ready to go to Balak).

5. Balaam arrives at Balak's place (Balaam responds to the attitude of Balak firmly; Balaam tells Balak that he shall speak the words that God puts in his mouth).

6. Balak slaughters oxen and sheep for Balaam.

From the chain of the topical verb, sub-topical verb, and topically-related verbs in section 2 ("seeing"—"uncovering"—"slaying"—"speaking [as the Lord commands]"—"slaughtering") it can be argued that the narrative of Num 22:22–40 is coherently centered on the verbs delivering the topicality. Accordingly, the topic of section 2 is that Balaam, on the way to Balak, encounters the angel of the Lord, who by uncovering Balaam's eyes and by threatening him with death equips him as a tool of the Lord. Thus he is able to proclaim that he shall speak the words as God commands before Balak.

It is important to consider that the chain of the topical verb, sub-topical verb, and topically-related verbs also demonstrates the inter-coherence between the two sections as well as the inner coherence within each section (Num 22:2–21 and Num 22:22–40). For the inter-coherence, a pattern

IMPLICATIONS OF THE BALAAM STORY

exists between the two sections in addition to their sharing of the topical, sub-topical, and topically-related verbs. The obstacle to Balaam's going occurs in episode 2 (God's disapproval of Balaam's going to Balak) of section 1 and in episode 4 (the angel of the Lord blocks Balaam's way to Balak) of section 2. Opposition also occurs in episode 3 (God's allowance of Balaam's going to Balak, with the request for speaking as he commands) of section 1 and in episode 5 (the allowance of the Lord for Balaam's going to Balak, with the request for speaking as he commands) of section 2.

This pattern reflects the same nuance regarding the matter of Balaam's going in pairs in the two sections "do not go"—"go to deliver the words of God" and implies that the two sections do not stand against each other. Further, this pattern renders the argument regarding whether and why God changed his mind about Balaam's going to Balak moot; although the matter regarding whether Balaam goes to Balak or not or whether God allows Balaam to go to Balak or not initially seems to be crucial, it is incidental in comparison to the fact of Balaam's speaking as God commands. The description of the attitudes of God and Balaam regarding the matter of Balaam's going to Balak functions to support and reveal the story's topicality, led by the topical and topically-related verbs.

There is another pattern between the issue of Balaam's going to Balak and the topically-related verbs ברך/ארר/קבב (blessing/cursing/cursing) and דבר/עשׂה (speaking/doing) in episodes 2 and 3 of section 1. God does not allow Balaam to go to Balak in episode 2, while God allows Balaam to go to Balak in episode 3. These opposite reactions of God seem to show that there is inconsistency between the two episodes as one narrative. However, there is a pattern to the reactions. God's allowing Balaam to go accompanies the topically-related verb of blessing and cursing ("you shall not curse the people, for they are blessed" in 22:12), while God's reaction of stopping Balaam's going utilizes the topically-related verbs of speaking and doing ("only the word which I speak to you shall you do" in 22:20). In spite of the seemingly opposite reactions of God regarding Balaam's going to Balak, the accompanying expressions support the coherence of the topicality by the presence of the two topically-related verbs. This pattern is consistent with my view that episodes 1 and 2 are under the control of the topicality of the Balaam story and develop the dramatic plot and message of the Balaam story.

Sections 1 and 2 share the common topic of "seeing" by the two characters of Balak and God. Balak sees what Israel had done to the Amorites and wishes to defeat her through cursing, whereas God prepares Balaam to see the vision of blessing toward Israel. In this phase, the shared common topic is conveyed mainly by "words/conversations" (the officials' delivering Balak's message to Balaam, Balaam's reply, and God's commandment on Balaam) among the characters in section 1, and by "actions/events" (the Lord's blocking Balaam's way, the donkey's speaking to Balaam, the Lord's uncovering Balaam's eyes, Balaam's encountering the threat of death, and Balaam's going to Balak) among the characters in section 2. The topically-related verb דבר/עשׂה (speaking/doing) is effectively disclosed with the double confirmation of "words" and "actions" in the two sections.

One of the most important topical elements in sections 1 and 2 is the presence of the topically-related verbs דבר/עשׂה (speaking/doing). The two verses in sections 1 and 2 are pivotal in each section because they include these topically-related verbs, דבר/עשׂה (speaking/doing): "Since these men have come to summon you, go with them, but do only what I tell you" (22:20) and "Go with the men, but speak only what I tell you" (22:35). These occurrences of the same critical topically-related verb in the two sections show that these two sections are intentionally woven together as a narrative. The intentionality is also revealed through the location of the verses. The same topical verses are located in the end of each section. Each concluding episode of sections 1 and 2 (episode 3 and episode 6) have the same topically-related verbs, דבר/עשׂה (speaking/doing). The verbs are used by the two topical main characters of God and Balaam in each concluding episode: "only the word which I speak to you shall you do" (22:20 in episode 3) and "the word that God puts in my mouth, that I shall speak" (22:38 in episode 6). Therefore, it is reasonable to conclude that the author designates them structurally to express the dramatic message of the narrative.

The same expressions of "speak (do) only what I will tell you" in the narrative part (sections 1 and 2) are repeated at the ends of the poetic collection. The topically-related verbs דבר/עשׂה (speaking/doing) echo at the ends of the three episodes in section 3: "must I not take care to speak what the Lord puts in my mouth?" (23:12, episode 7), "Did I not tell you, saying, 'all that the Lord speaks, that I must do'?" (23:26, episode 8), and "what the Lord speaks, that will I speak" (24:13, episode 9). The appearance of these topically-related verbs at the end of each poetic part supports my argument that the topicality of section 3 develops that of sections 1 and 2. Accordingly, the poetic parts of section 3 should be understood in the same topical frame under the topically-related verbs דבר/עשׂה (speaking/doing). This topical frame with the topically-related verbs differentiates the first three oracles, in which the verbs are at the ends, from the following oracles and designates them the main oracles in section 3. As a result, the pattern of the topically-related verbs דבר/עשׂה (speaking/doing), which ends the two sections of the narrative and the first three main poetic parts in the last section, strengthens the intended topicality of the Balaam story.

The verb of "speaking" is uniquely present in all sections. That is, the verb conveys a message throughout the entire story. However, the verb's voice becomes stronger as the episodes progress until the end of the story.

Relationship between Sections 1 and 2 (Prosaic Parts), and Section 3 (Poetic Collections): The Topical Congruency between the Two Genres in the Balaam Story

The analytical study of chapter 2 reveals that the prosaic parts (sections 1 and 2) and the poetic collections (section 3) of the Balaam story are related topically, coherently, and systematically. The close relationship between the two genres is demonstrated by the topicality established through the topical verbs (sub-topical verbs), the topical key phrases determined by the topically-related verbs, and the topical verbs (sub-topical and topically-related verbs), illuminating the chiastic structure and the tensions among the topical main characters in the Balaam story.

The work of section 2 is prominent in the structure of the whole story because section 2 as the body of the Balaam story is the core of the chiastic structure. Considering section 2 as the core makes the prosaic introduction (section 1) and the poetic conclusion (section 3) symmetrical to each other. Section 2's inclusion of the topical theme of death intensifies the topicality of sections 1 and 3. Accordingly, the Balaam story generates the topicality in the introductory prosaic parts of section 1, echoes and amplifies the topicality through the climactic section 2, and concludes the topicality in the poetic collections of section 3.

The prominent connection between the prosaic parts and the poetic collection is disclosed through the chiastic structure outlined in chapter 2. The exact matching points between section 1 and 3 are as below:

Who Is the True Seer Driven by God?

Table 16. Verbal Chiasm in Num 22–24

	Section 1		Section 3
E. 1	The topical verb ראה (to see) appears at the beginning of the Balaam story.	E. 9 (Balaam's third and final oracles)	The topical verb ראה (to see) ends the Balaam story.
	The language of blessing and cursing begins in the story.		The language of blessing and cursing ends in the story.
	The will and message of the Lord regarding the topicality of "seeing" are not revealed yet.		The will and message of the Lord regarding the topicality of "seeing" are revealed completely and successfully.
	Balak sees all that Israel had done to the Amorites.		Balaam sees what Israel will do in the future.
E. 2	Balaam asks God how he should respond to Balak's request for cursing Israel.	E. 8 (Balaam's second oracle)	Balaam confirms how he has to respond regarding Balak's request for cursing Israel.
	God instructs Balaam not to curse Israel because they are blessed.		God answers Balaam not to curse Israel because Israel is blessed.
	Balaam refuses to go with the officials of Moab.		Then, Balaam refuses to tell Balak anything except for all that the Lord speaks.
E. 3	Balak again asks for Balaam to curse Israel.	E. 7 (Balaam's first oracle)	Balak asks for Balaam to curse Israel in the presence of Balak.
	Balaam demonstrates that he must do as the Lord commands.		Balaam demonstrates that he will only speak what the Lord shows.
	God commands Balaam to speak as he commands.		God commands Balaam to speak to Balak as he commands.
	God lets Balaam go with the officials of Balak.		God lets Balaam go and speak to Balak.

Each point introduced above consists of the topical, sub-topical, and topically-related verbs. The points in the introductory section 1 echo, develop, and complete the topicality in the concluding section 3. This examination suggests that the prosaic part of section 1 is organically connected to the poetic collection of section 3. This intended structure of the Balaam text expresses the topicality effectively and dramatically through the symmetry of the prosaic and poetic genres.

Section 3, which is the final section, also has a pattern showing that the prosaic parts (section 1 and 2) and the poetic collections (section 3) have topical congruency. The topical and topically-related verbs occur intensively and form a pattern in the final section.

Episodes 7, 8, and 9 in section 3 have the same patterns of topical and topically-related verbs:

Implications of the Balaam Story

(1) Balaam sees Israel.

(2) Balaam sacrifices a bull and a ram.

(3) The Lord lets Balaam speak to Balak.

(4) Balaam speaks what the Lord commands.

(5) Balaam blesses Israel.

(6) Balaam, in the presence of Balak, confirms that he speaks as the Lord commands.

All the topical and topically-related verbs in the poetic collections of section 3 appear in the prosaic parts of sections 1 and 2. The topicality through the verbs in the prosaic parts is connected to the topicality through the same verbs in the poetic collections. Further, the feature that all the topical and topically-related verbs occur together intensively in the final section emphasizes the conclusion of the final section as well as shows that the verbs begin the topicality at the heading of the story (prosaic part), develops the topicality as the story goes (prosaic part), and concludes the topicality as the story ends (poetic part). The topicality of the story that began in and developed through the prosaic parts ends in the poetic collections in order to disclose the message and intention of the story dramatically and effectively. This organization of the topicality through the two genres (prosaic parts and poetic collections) shows that the Balaam story has a well-woven unity as well as that there is topical congruency between the two genres.

The Message, Intension, and Theological Implications of the Balaam Story

The chiastic structure (pages 106–108]) and diagrams (diagram 1) of the topical, sub-topical, and topically-related verbs in chapter 2 show how topicality is formed and how the Balaam story in Num 22–24 is tightly woven, clearly conveying the role of Balaam through the unity between 22:2–21 and 22:22–40 and the topical congruency between the prosaic parts and poetic collections.

The development of the topicality and the tensional relationship among the main topical characters of the story revealed by the structure and diagrams manifest that the Balaam story in Num 22–24 has a dramatic plot that includes an introduction, rising action, climax, falling action, and resolution. The plot of the story is expressed effectively by the combination of the topical (and sub-topical and topically-related) verbs and the main topical characters. The topical development in that combination makes the message and intention of the story obvious and delivers the plot of the story to readers.

The main topical characters, Balak, Balaam, and God, around the topical, sub-topical, and topically-related verbs, initiate the topicality of the Balaam story. Balak, who occurs as the first topical character in the heading, cannot caccess the topicality, as he is distinguished from the active main topical characters, Balaam and God. He, occurring with the verbs, hovers around the other characters to share the core of the topicality, but does not go into the core zone of the topicality. He sees what Israel had done to the Amorites, but cannot see the vision of the Lord. He does not experience the Lord opening his eyes. He cannot speak as the Lord commands. He wants to hear words of cursing toward Israel, but cannot do so. He cannot become a tool of the Lord through the experience of death, even though he stands closer to the place of the sacrifice.

Balaam, who is the most frequent character with the verbs, has access to the core of the topicality of the story. He receives the mission to deliver blessings toward Israel by God. He experiences the Lord opening his eyes and he encounters the threat of death from the angel of the Lord, which leads to his readiness to see the vision of the Lord and to speak as the Lord commands before Balak. He receives a word and vision of blessing toward Israel, and speaks, as a tool of the Lord, what he puts in his mouth.

God, who is the giver of this word and vision, controls the topicality of the story. He appears before Balaam and commands him what to do. He lets Balaam know that he has decided to bless Israel. He almost kills Balaam on the way to Balak in order to make him ready as his tool for the mission to see and speak the vision and the word of the Lord. He comes to Balaam to provide the oracles and to let him speak the blessing toward Israel as he has commanded, whenever Balaam (with Balak) sees the encampment of Israel and sacrifices a bull and a ram.

The development and result of the tension among the three characters contrasts the active status of Balaam and God to the semi-active status of Balak toward the topicality. In the beginning of the story, episodes 1 and 2 do not reveal the different status of the three main characters' topicality: active vs. semi-active. However, as the story continues, the active status of Balaam and God is distinguished from the semi-active status of Balak

Implications of the Balaam Story

around the topicality regarding "seeing" the vision of the Lord. The topical tension between Balaam and God gradually disappears and becomes extinct after the climax, in which Balaam is ready as a tool of the Lord, as the active status of God and Balaam to the topicality becomes prominent and readers are able to recognize God and Balaam as the most important topical main characters, whereas the topical tension between Balaam and Balak becomes increasingly bad after the climax as Balak's semi-active status to the topicality grows in strength; thus readers can grasp that Balak fails to rank with God and Balaam as the most important topical main character.

As a unified and consistent text, the Balaam story in Num 22–24, topically defined through the combination of the topical/sub-topical/topically-related verbs and the main topical characters, exhibits a specific message and intention. After seeing what Israel had done to the Amorites, Balak wants to defeat Israel through Balaam's cursing of Israel. Balak is dependent on Balaam to curse Israel because he is not personally able to curse Israel and feels that this is the task of a professional person. God wants to bless Israel, however, and decides to send Balaam to Balak to deliver a message stating this. Between Balak and God, Balaam consistently demonstrates that he will do (speak) as the Lord commands. On Balaam's way to Balak to fulfill God's mission, Balaam receives a threat of danger of death from an angel of the Lord. Through this experience, Balaam recognizes that this is a mission he must fulfill at the risk of his life, and he needs to be ready as a tool of God for this mission. At the first meeting with Balak, Balaam clarifies his attitude to speak as the Lord commands. After that, Balaam sees Israel and the vision of the Lord and speaks a blessing toward Israel as the Lord puts the words in his mouth through poetic oracles. Fulfilling the mission, Balaam discloses his status as a tool of the Lord and his intimacy with him. On the other hand, Balak, who should be dependent on Balaam for cursing Israel, recognizes that Israel is destined for the blessing of the Lord, and he becomes more distant from Balaam regarding the wish to curse Israel. Finally, the Balaam story in Num 22–24 conveys that (1) God decides to bless Israel even though Balak wants to curse her, (2) God makes Balaam his tool to deliver that message to Balak, and (3) Balaam completes the mission before Balak and proclaims the blessing of God toward Israel. This message and intention of the Balaam story is revealed dramatically by the unity between section 1 (Num 22:2–21) and section 2 (22:22–40) and organized systematically by the cooperation of the topical (and sub-topical and topically-related) verbs and the topically-related main characters.

Who Is the True Seer Driven by God?

As a result of the growth and development of the topicality through the topical, sub-topical, and topically-related verbs, the Balaam story discloses certain prominent theological implications.

First, God is sovereign over his people and other nations. As the most important main character, God decides to protect his people, Israel; delivers a message of blessing towards Israel through a foreigner, Balaam; and controls the fate of other nations, including Balak's. God is the one who guides his people, Israel, to the plains of Moab, inspires Balak, the king of Moab, with awe for Israel, appears to and sends a messenger of his choice for the mission (Balaam), prepares his perfect tool for the mission, shows this messenger his vision, and lets him speak as he commands. God has the controlling power over Balaam and Balak as well as Israel and other nations. The Balaam story is not interested in whether or not Balaam is a true prophet of the Lord or whether Balaam reflects a good or bad character. The Balaam story is mainly interested in the sovereignty of God, rather than Balaam, who is a mere tool of God. According to the story, God is the only sovereign of Israel, other nations, and Balaam and Balak.

Second, God shows grace toward Israel. In the Balaam story, Israel does not appear in any scene. Nonetheless, the Balaam story is punctuated by God's will for the blessing of Israel in the prosaic parts and Balaam's proclamations of the blessing toward Israel from God in the poetic collections. The journey of Israel in the book of Numbers shows that Israel does not deserve the blessing of God because the people of Israel constantly complain about their lives in the wilderness and disobey the words of God. However, God protects Israel and announces the blessing of Israel to Balaam through this special message, which is not delivered directly to the one who is the beneficiary of the blessing but is heard through a foreigner. That God would let other nations know the blessing of his people, Israel, appears to be an intense expression of his grace. According to the Balaam story, Israel is not aware of the fact that God blesses her before other nations. The fact that God discloses the blessing of Israel to third parties, Balaam, Balak, and other nations, alludes to his self-confident and one-sided grace. Therefore, this unconditional grace of God should be viewed as an important aspect of the theology of the Balaam story and the book of Numbers.

Third, God's will to bless Israel is unchanging and everlasting. The grace of God mentioned above is expressed by the topic of "blessing and cursing." The topic of "blessing and cursing" is also an important theme in

Implications of the Balaam Story

the book of Genesis.[4] Specifically, the phrase of "blessing and cursing" in the book of Numbers parallels that of "blessing and cursing" in the book of Genesis: "he whom you bless is blessed, and he whom you curse is cursed" (Num 22:6); "blessed are those who bless you, and cursed are those who curse you" (Num 24:9); "I will bless those who bless you, and him who dishonors you I will curse" (Gen 12:3); and "Cursed be everyone who curses you, and blessed be everyone who blesses you" (Gen 27:29). The phrase in Num 22:6 from the saying of Balak does not have the same meaning as in the other three phrases above. The phrases of Num 24:9 and Gen 27:29 reflect on the original phrase of "blessing and cursing" in Gen 12:3.

This parallel between the phrases of "blessing" and "cursing" in the books of Genesis and Numbers shows that God's blessing toward Israel in the Balaam story results from the original blessing of God toward Abraham. God originally blesses Abraham, and the blessing extends to the Abrahamic community: "and in you all the families of the earth shall be blessed" (Gen 12:3b). The same blessing, through the phrase of "blessing and cursing," is connected to Jacob by Isaac (Gen 27:29). The same blessing also reaches the people of Israel, that is, the Mosaic community, including them as recipients of Isaac's blessing in Gen 27:29. The theological image of God's blessing toward the people of Israel through Balaam's oracle in the book of Numbers mirrors God's original blessing toward Abraham and Jacob in the book of Genesis. In the book of Numbers, through the Balaam story, God proclaims the blessing toward the people of Israel revealing God's guidance on the Mosaic community as well as the Abrahamic community. In spite of the Israelites' failure to obey God in the wilderness, God will neither curse his people nor cease to lead Israel.[5]

Fourth, God makes his agent ready to be used as his tool for a mission. Balaam seems to be employed as a foreign diviner rather than an Israelite prophet. He never plans to bless or curse the people of Israel voluntarily. Instead, God uses Balaam as his tool to deliver a message from him. Balaam's successful completion of God's mission was possible when he was ready

---

4. Alexander, *From Paradise to the Promised Land*, 249. Alexander mentions that "he [Balaam] echoes briefly the promises made earlier to the patriarchs in Genesis: 'Who can count the dust of Jacob' (23:10; cf. Gen 13:16; 15:5); 'The LORD their God is with them' (23:21; cf. Gen 17:8); 'May those who bless you be blessed and those who curse you be cursed' (24:9; cf. 23:8, 20; Gen 12:3); 'A star will come out of Jacob; a scepter will rise out of Israel' (24:17; cf. Gen 17:6, 16; 49:10)."

5. Cole, *Numbers*, 364.

to be the tool of God.[6] In order to become a perfect tool for God, Balaam experiences the meeting with the angel of the Lord at the risk of his life. The theological image of God preparing Balaam as his tool or agent for a given mission by the special event of facing death parallels the image of Moses in the book of Exodus (Exod 4:24–26). The role of Balaam as the tool of God for Israel is the same as that of Moses for Israel. God makes his tool completely ready for his mission and commits him to working for the mission of God.

Last, Balaam sees a dual-purposed vision of God. In the beginning of the story, Balaam has a duty to see and speak the vision of God, which is a blessing toward Israel. But, at the end, Balaam sees the future fate of Israel and the doomed fate of other people groups as well as the blessing of Israel. The dual-purposed vision of God is seeing the welfare of the Israelite people on the one hand and seeing the demise of Moab and other peoples on the other hand. This dual-purposed vision works in concert with the tensions between God, Balaam, and Balak. As the tension between Balaam and God gradually disappears and Balaam comes closer to seeing the vision of God, he can see the vision of Israel's blessing and the future welfare of the Israelite people. As the tension between Balaam and Balak gradually increases, and Balaam comes closer to seeing the vision of God, he also sees the vision of Moab and other nations' collapse. As a result, Balak's wish to curse Israel after his seeing what Israel had done to the Amorites is not completed, and Balak sees even the unwanted consequences through Balaam's vision. The Balaam story, through Balaam, discloses the contrasting fates of God's people and other nations in the vision of God.

---

6. Sakenfeld, *Journeying with God*, 130. Sakenfeld mentions that "God commands Balaam to speak only what God tells him to say, and only through Balaam's perfect obedience will King Balak be challenged and Israel be blessed (e.g., Num. 22:20, 35) . . . The seer is simply the vehicle for uttering the word that God wants uttered, and so he 'must' speak oracles of blessing (e.g., 22:38)."

Conclusion

I HAVE EXAMINED THE Balaam story in Num 22–24 using the method of text linguistic and literary analysis, and have concluded that (1) the role of Balaam is as a mere tool of God who fulfills his mission to deliver a message of blessing to Israel; (2) there is a topical unity between Num 22:2–21 and 22:22–40; (3) there is also a topical congruency between the prose section and the poetic collection; (4) therefore, the Balaam story is organized as a united and consistent story, and as such reveals certain theological implications of the Balaam story in Num 22–24. My method for this study has operated from the standpoint that the topical verb in the heading of the text co-works with the sub-topical and topically-related verbs to develop the topicality of the story, which together reveal the message and intention of the text. The combination of the verbs and the characters associated with the verbs is vital for disclosing the topicality of the text effectively. I believe this method effectively resolves the textual problems raised in the introduction to my dissertation, helps to elucidates a clear message and intention, and supports the notion that the story has been carefully crafted as a unified, coherent whole. The uniqueness and contribution of this study is in regards to its ability to analyze linguistic features of a text; more specifically, to apply a text linguistic and literary theory that is able to reveal the meaning of a text along with its theological implications, which are based on the intentions of the text.

As a result of our examination of topicality in the whole Balaam story in Num 22–24, the answer to the question "Who is the true seer driven by God?" is obviously Balaam. Balaam is the true seer; he remains the active main topical character through the topicality of the topical verb ראה right to the end of the story. Balaam is the true seer. Driven and led by God and the one who actually saw what God allows, he practiced what God commands.

Bibliography

Abegg, Martin G., et al. *The Dead Sea Scrolls Bible: The Oldest Known Bible, Translated for the First Time into English*. New York: HarperCollins, 1999.

Albright, W. F. "The Oracles of Balaam." *JBL* 63 (2010) 207–33.

Alexander, T. Desmond. *From Paradise to the Promised Land: An Introduction to the Pentateuch*. Carlisle, UK: Paternoster, 2002.

Alter, Robert. *The Art of Biblical Narrative*. 2nd ed. New York: Basic, 2011.

———. "Balaam and the Ass: An Excerpt from a New Translation of the 'Five Books of Moses.'" *The Kenyon Review* 26 (2004) 6–32.

Ashley, Timothy R. *The Book of Numbers*. Grand Rapids, MI: Eerdmans, 1993.

Bailey, Lloyd R. *Leviticus-Numbers*. Macon, GA: Smyth & Helwys, 2005.

Baskin, J. R. "Origen on Balaam: The Dilemma of the Unworthy Prophet." *Vigiliae Christianae* 37 (1983) 22–35.

Begg, C. T. "Balaam's Talking Ass (Num 22,21–35): Three Retellings of Her Story." *Annali Di Storia Dell'esegesi* 24 (2007) 207–28.

ben Meir, Samuel. *Rashbam's Commentary on Leviticus and Numbers: An Annotated Translation*. Translated by Martin I. Lockshin. Providence, RI: Brown Judaic Studies, 2001.

Booth, Wayne C. *A Rhetoric of Irony*. Chicago, IL: University of Chicago Press, 1974.

Boyce, Richard N. *Leviticus and Numbers*. Louisville, KY: Westminster John Knox, 2008.

Brown, Gillian, and George Yule. *Discourse Analysis*. Cambridge: Cambridge University Press, 1983.

Brueggemann, Walter. "The Book of Exodus." In *The New Interpreter's Bible: General Articles & Introduction, Commentary, and Reflections for Each Book of the Bible, Including the Apocryphal/Deuterocanonical Books in Twelve Volumes*, edited by Neil M. Alexander, 1:677–981. 12 vols. Nashville, TN: Abingdon, 1994.

———. *Theology of the Old Testament: Testimony, Dispute, Advocacy*. Minneapolis, MN: Fortress, 1997.

Budd, Philip J. *Numbers*. Waco, TX: Word, 1984.

Buth, Randall. "Word Order in the Verbless Clause: A Generative-Functional Approach." In *The Verbless Clause in Biblical Hebrew: Linguistic Approaches*, edited by C. Miller, 79–108. Winona Lake, IN: Eisenbrauns, 1999.

Campbell, A. F., and M. A. O'Brien. *Sources of the Pentateuch: Texts, Introductions and Annotations*. Minneapolis, MN: Augsburg, 1993.

Childs, Brevard S. *Introduction to the Old Testament as Scripture*. Philadelphia, PA: Fortress, 1979.

Bibliography

Clark, Ira. "Balaam's Ass: Suture or Structure?" In *Literary Interpretations of Biblical Narratives*, edited by Kenneth R. R. Gros Louis et al., 2:137–44. 2 vols. Nashville, TN: Abingdon, 1982.

Coats, G. W. "The Way of Obedience: Traditio-historical and hermeneutical reflections on the Balaam story." *Semeia* 24 (1982) 53–79.

Cole, R. Dennis. *Numbers*. Nashville, TN: Broadman & Holman, 2000.

Davies, Eryl W. *Numbers: Based on the Revised Standard Version*. London: Marshall Pickering, 1995.

De Beaugrande, Robert, and Wolfgang U. Dressler. *Introduction to Text Linguistics*. London: Longman, 1981.

Dijkstra, Meindert. "Is Balaam Also among the Prophets?" *JBL* 114 (1995) 43–64.

———. "The Geography of the Story of Balaam: Synchronic Reading as a Help to Date a Biblical Text." In *Synchronic or Diachronic? A Debate on Method in Old Testament Exegesis*, edited by Johannes C. de Moor, 72–97. Leiden: Brill, 1995.

Dooley, Robert A. "Explorations in Discourse Topicality." Electronic Working Papers of SIL. 2007. https://www.sil.org/resources/archives/7828.

Douglas, Mary. *In the Wilderness: The Doctrine of Defilement in the Book of Numbers*. Oxford: Oxford University Press, 2001.

Dozeman, Thomas. "The Book of Numbers." In *The New Interpreter's Bible: General Articles & Introduction, Commentary, and Reflections for Each Book of the Bible, Including the Apocryphal/Deuterocanonical Books in Twelve Volumes*, edited by Neil M. Alexander, 2:1–268. 12 vols. Nashville, TN: Abingdon, 1994.

Floor, Sebastiaan Jonathan. "From Information Structure, Topic and Focus, to Theme in Biblical Hebrew Narrative." PhD diss., University of Stellenbosch, 2004.

Frevel, Christian. "The Book of Numbers—Formation, Composition, and Interpretation of a Late Part of the Torah. Some Introductory Remarks." In *Torah and the Book of Numbers*, edited by Christian Frevel et al., 1–37. Tübingen: Mohr Siebeck, 2013.

García Martínez, Florentino, and Eibert J. C. Tigchelaar. *The Dead Sea Scrolls Study Edition*. Leiden: Brill, 2000.

Givón, T. *Topic Continuity in Discourse: A Quantitative Cross-Language Study*. Cover endorsement. Philadelphia, PA: John Benjamins, 1983.

Goldingay, John. *Numbers and Deuteronomy for Everyone*. Louisville, KY: Westminster John Knox, 2010.

Gray, George Buchanan. *A Critical and Exegetical Commentary on Numbers*. Edinburgh: T. & T. Clark, 1903.

Greene, John T. *Balaam and His Interpreters: A Hermeneutical History of the Balaam Traditions*. Atlanta, GA: Scholars, 1992.

Heimerdinger, Jean-Marc. *Topic, Focus and Foreground in Ancient Hebrew Narratives*. Sheffield, UK: Sheffield Academic, 1999.

Jeanrond, Werner. *Theological Hermeneutics: Development and Significance*. New York: Crossroad, 1991.

Jones, Spencer A. "Balaam, Pagan Prophet of God: A Commentary on Greek Numbers 22.1–21." In *The SBL Commentary on the Septuagint: An Introduction*, edited by Dirk Büchner, 123–67. Atlanta, GA: SBL, 2017.

Kamp, Albert H. *Inner Worlds: A Cognitive-Linguistic Approach to the Book of Jonah*. Boston, MA: Brill, 2004.

Kelley, Page H., et al. *The Masorah of Biblia Hebraica Stuttgartensia: Introduction and Annotated Glossary*. Grand Rapids, MI: Eerdmans, 1998.

Bibliography

Knierim, Rolf P., and George W. Coats. *Numbers*. Grand Rapids, MI: Eerdmans, 2005.
Köhler, Ludwig, and Walter Baumgartner. "ירט." *HALOT*, 1:438.
———. "עלה." *HALOT*, 1:830.
Layton, S. C. "Whence Comes Balaam: Num 22:5 Revisited." *Biblica* 73 (1992) 32–61.
Lee, Won W. *Punishment and Forgiveness in Israel's Migratory Campaign*. Grand Rapids, MI: Eerdmans, 2003.
Levine, Baruch A. *Numbers 21–36: A New Translation with Introduction and Commentary*. New York: Doubleday, 2000.
Longacre, Robert E. "Discourse Perspective on the Hebrew Verb: Affirmation and Restatement." In *Linguistics and Biblical Hebrew*, edited by Walter R. Bodine, 177–89. Winona Lake, IN: Eisenbrauns, 1992.
———. "The Discourse Structure of the Flood Narrative." *SBLSP*, 235–62.
———. *Joseph: A Story of Divine Providence. A Text Theoretical and Textlinguistic Analysis of Genesis 37 and 39–48*. Winona Lake, IN: Eisenbrauns, 1989.
Lutzky, H. C. "Ambivalence toward Balaam." *VT* 49 (1999) 421–25.
Mann, Thomas W. *The Book of the Torah: The Narrative Integrity of the Pentateuch*. Eugene, OR: Cascade, 2013.
Milgrom, Jacob. *Numbers: The Traditional Hebrew Text with the New JPS Translation*. Philadelphia, PA: Jewish Publication Society, 1990.
Miller, William T. *A Compact Study of Numbers*. Eugene, OR: Wipf & Stock, 2013.
Moore, Michael S. *The Balaam Traditions: Their Character and Development*. Atlanta, GA: Scholars, 1990.
Moyer, Clinton John. "Literary and Linguistic Studies in Sefer Bilʻam (Num 22–24)." PhD diss., Cornell University, 2009.
———. "Who Is the Prophet, and Who the Ass? Role-Reversing Interludes and the Unity of the Balaam Narrative (Numbers 22–24)." *JSOT* 37 (2012) 167–83.
Noth, Martin. *Numbers: A Commentary*. Philadelphia, PA: Westminster, 1986.
Notarius, Tania. "Poetic Discourse and the Problem of Verbal Tenses in the Oracles of Balaam." *Hebrew Studies* 49 (2008) 55–86.
Olson, Dennis T. *Numbers*. Louisville, KY: John Knox, 1996.
Provan, Iain, et al. *A Biblical History of Israel*. Louisville, KY: Westminster John Knox, 2003.
Robar, Elizabeth. *The Verb and the Paragraph in Biblical Hebrew: A Cognitive-Linguistic Approach*. Leiden: Brill, 2014.
Robker, Jonathan Miles. "The Balaam Narrative in the Pentateuch/Hexateuch/Enneateuch." In *Torah and the Book of Numbers*, edited by Christian Frevel et al., 334–66. Tübingen: Mohr Siebeck, 2013.
Safren, J. D. "Balaam and Abraham." *VT* 38 (1988) 105–13.
Sakenfeld, Katharine Doob. *Journeying with God: A Commentary on the Book of Numbers*. Grand Rapids, MI: Eerdmans, 1995.
Sals, Ulrike. "The Hybrid Story of Balaam (Numbers 22–24): Theology for the Diaspora in the Torah." *BI* 16 (2008) 315–35.
Savelle, Charles H. "Canonical and Extracanonical Portraits of Balaam." *Bibliotheca Sacra* 166 (2009) 387–404.
Savran, G. "Beastly Speech: Intertextuality, Balaam's Ass and the Garden of Eden." *JSOT* 19 (1994) 33–55.
Scott, William R. *A Simplified Guide to* BHS: *Critical Apparatus, Masora, Accents, Unusual Letters & Other Markings*. North Richland Hills, TX: Bibal, 1987.

Bibliography

Spero, S. "Moses Wrote His Book and the Portion of Balaam." *JBQ* 41 (2013) 193–200.
Stuart, Douglas K. *Exodus*. Nashville, TN: Broadman & Holman, 2006.
Stubbs, David L. *Numbers*. Grand Rapids, MI: Brazos, 2009.
Talstra, Eep. "Text Linguistics: Biblical Hebrew." In *Encyclopedia of Hebrew Language and Linguistics*, edited by Geoffrey Khan, 3:755–60. 4 vols. Leiden: Brill, 2013.
Tosato, Angelo. "The Literary Structure of the First Two Poems of Balaam (Num 23:7–10, 18–24)." *VT* 29 (1979) 98–106.
Tov, Emanuel. "A Didactic Approach to the Biblical Dead Sea Scrolls." In *Celebrating the Dead Sea Scrolls: A Canadian Collection*, edited by Peter W. Flint et al., 173–98. Atlanta, GA: SBL, 2011.
Van der Merwe, C. H. J. "Review of J.-M. Heimerdinger, *Topic, Focus and Foreground in Ancient Hebrew Narrative*." *Biblica* 81 (2000) 574–78.
Van Seters, John. "From Faithful Prophet to Villain: Observations on the Tradition History of the Balaam Story." In *A Biblical Itinerary: In Search of Method, Form, and Content: Essays in Honor of Geroge W. Coats*, edited by Eugene E. Carpenter, 126–32. JSOTSup. Sheffield, UK: Sheffield Academic, 1997.
———. *The Life of Moses: The Yahwist as Historian in Exodus-Numbers*. Louisville, KY: Westminster/John Knox, 1994.
Walsh, Jerome T. *Style and Structure in Biblical Hebrew Narrative*. Collegeville, MN: Liturgical, 2001.
Way, Kenneth. "Animals in the Prophetic World: Literary Reflections on Numbers 22 and 1 Kings 13." *JSOT* 34 (2009) 47–62.
Wenham, Gordon J. *Exploring the Old Testament: Pentateuch*. Downers Grove, IL: InterVarsity, 2002.
———. *Numbers: An Introduction and Commentary*. Leicester: InterVarsity, 1981.
Yahuda, A. S. "The Name of Balaam's Homeland." *JBL* 64 (1945) 547–51.
Zannoni, A. E. "Balaam: International Seer / Wizard Prophet." *Saint Luke's Journal of Theology* 22 (1978) 5–19.

Name Index

Abegg, Martin G., 2n3
Albright, W. F., 3n9, 22n2
Alexander, T. Desmond, 127n4
Alter, Robert, 1n1, 22n3, 23n4, 34n30, 41n40
Ashley, Timothy R., xviin2, xx, xxn19, 2n2, 4, 4nn12–13, 6n19, 9, 9n26, 15, 15nn60–61, 18, 18n77, 20, 20n83, 46n46, 47n47, 48n51, 64n69, 116n1

Bailey, Lloyd R., xviin1, 47n47
Bar-Efrat, Shimon, 34n30
Baskin, J. R., 1n1
Begg, C. T., 1n1
Booth, Wayne C., xviiin5
Boyce, Richard N., xviin3
Brown, Gillian, 28n19, 32n28
Brueggemann Walter, 31, 31nn25–26, 84n77
Buber, Martin, 34, 34n30
Budd, Philip J., xviin4, 9, 9n27, 10n29, 11, 11nn33–37
Buth, Randall, xxin20-21, 24n10

Campbell, A. F., 3n4
Childs, Brevard S., 47n47, 48, 48n50
Clark, Ira, 46n46, 59n55, 91n81
Coats, George W., xviin1, xviin2, xx, xxn17, 1n1, 12, 12n44, 16, 16n64, 17–18, 18nn74–76, 47n47, 116n1
Cole, R. Dennis, xviin3, xxn15, 6n19, 8, 8nn22–23, 12, 12nn42–43, 46n46, 127n5

Dante, 23n4
Davies, Eryl W., xviin4, 9n27
De Beaugrande, Robert, 23n5
Dijkstra, Meiddert, 1n1, 3, 3n9
Douglas, Mary, xviin2, xix, xixn9, 1n1, 13, 13n49
Dozeman, Thomas, xxn15, 3, 4n10, 6n19
Dressler, Wolfgang U., 23n5

Eliot, T. S., 22n3

Floor, Sebastiaan Jonathan, 25, 25n12
Fokkelman, Jan, 23n4
Frevel, Christian, 4, 4n14, 5, 5n15

Garcia Martinez, Florentino, 2n3
Givón, T., 24n10, 28n19, 29n22
Goldingay, John, xviin3
Gray, George Buchanan, 3, 3n4, 3n5, 9, 9n27, 10n29, 13, 13nn50–57
Greene, John T., 1n1, 3n4, 6n19, 9n25

Heimerdinger, Jean-Marc, xviii, xx–xxii, xxin22–23, xxiin24-25, 2, 21n1, 24, 24nn7–9, 24n10, 25n11, 25n12, 26n13, 26n14, 27, 27nn15–16, 28nn17–18, 28n19, 29nn20–21, 32–33, 32nn27–28, 33n25, 34n31, 35–36, 35nn32–34, 36n35, 43, 45, 45n44, 46, 46n45, 93n82
Holmstedt, 24n10

135

Name Index

Jeanrond, Werner, 24n6
Jones, Spencer A., 22n2

Kamp, Albert H., 30n24
Keenan, 28n19
Kelley, Page H., 47n48
Knierim, Rolf P., xviin1, xviin2, xx, xxn17, 12n44, 16, 16n64, 18nn74–76, 47n47, 116n1
Kroeze, 24n10

Layton, S. C., 1n1
Lee, Won W., 9n27, 14, 14n56
Levine, Baruch A., xviin1, xviin2, xix, xixn14, xxn15, 4, 4n11, 6, 6n19, 7n21, 8, 9, 9n27, 16, 16nn66–68, 17, 19, 19nn79–80, 47n47, 116n1
Lutzky, H. C., 1n1

Maier, 9n27
Mann, Thomas W., xviin2, xix, xixn12–13, 14, 14n57
Milgrom, Jacob, xviin1, xviin2, xx, xxn15, xxn18, 6n19, 9, 13–14, 13n52, 14nn53–55, 16, 16n69, 17, 17nn70–73, 19, 19nn81–82, 46n46, 47n47, 116n1
Miller, William T., 80n74
Moore, Michael S., 1n1, 6n19, 6n20, 8n24, 14, 14nn58–59
Moyer, Clinton John, 1n1, 34n30

Naudé, 24n10
Notarius, Tania, xviin2, xix, xixn7, 1n1, 15n62, 22n2
Noth, Martin, xviin4, 3, 3n4, 3nn6–8, 9, 9n27, 10, 10n30, 11nn31–32

O'Brien, M. A., 3n4
Olson, Dennis T., xviin1, xviin2, xviin3, xix, xixn10–11, 9, 11, 11n38, 12nn39–41, 47n47

Provan, Iain, 22n3, 23n4, 41n39

Robar, Elizabeth, 30n23
Robker, Jonathan Miles, 5, 5nn16–18, 6
Rosenbaum, 24n10

Safren, J. D., 1n1, 37n36
Sakenfeld, Katharine Doob, 128n6
Sals, Ulrike, 1n1
Savelle, Charles H., xviin3, 10n28
Savran, G., 1n1
Schieffelin, 28n19
Scott, William R., 47n48
Shakespeare, William, 23n4
Shimasaki, 24n10
Spero, S., 1n1
Stuart, Douglas K., 84n77
Stubbs, David L., xviin3

Talstra, Eep, 23n5, 24n10
Tigchelaar. Eibert J. C., 2n3
Tolstoy, 23n4
Tomlin, 28, 32
Tosato, Angelo, 1n1, xviin2, xixn8, 16n65, 22n2
Tov, Emanuel, 2n3

Van der Merwe, C. H. J., 24n10
Van Seters, John, xviin2, xviin4, xx, xxn16, 3n4, 6n19, 15, 16n63, 19, 19n78, 47n47

Walsh, Jerome T., 41n38, 42n41, 58n55
Way, Kenneth, 1n1, 22n2
Weinrich, 30n24
Wenham, Gordon J., 9, 10n27, 12–13, 13nn45–48, 46n46

Yahuda, A. S., 1n1
Yee, Gale, 22n3
Yule, George, 28n19, 32n28

Zannoni, A. E., 1n1

Scripture Index

OLD TESTAMENT

Genesis

	127
12:3	127, 127n4
12:3b	127
13:16	127n4
15:5	127n4
17:6	127n4
17:8	127n4
17:16	127n4
20:7	37n36
22	26n13, 27n15, 32, 33n29, 83
22:1	37
22:1–19	37, 37n36, 43, 83
22:3	37n36, 38
22:4	38
22:6	38
22:7–8	38
22:8	38
22:11	37n36
22:13	38
22:14	38
23:3	37n36
27:29	127
49:10	127n4

Exodus

4:16	84n77
4:18	84
4:18–19	84
4:18–26	83n77, 84, 84n77, 85n77
4:20	84
4:21	84
4:21–23	84
4:24	84
4:24–26	84n77, 128
4:25	84n77
4:25–26	84
4:26	84
13:15	82n75

Numbers

	4, 5, 5n16, 47, 127
1:1	47n49
2:1	47n49
3:1	47n49
4:17	47n49
4:21	47n49
5:11	47n49
6:1	47n49
6:22	47n49
7:48	47n49
8:1	47n49
10:1	47n49
11:16	47n49
11:21	47n49
11–36	2n3
12:16	48n52
13:1	47n49
13:3	47n49
13–14	xix
14:11	47n49

Scripture Index

Numbers (*continued*)

15	xix
15:1	47n49
16:1	47n49
17:16	47n49
19:1	47n49
20:14	47n49
21	49
21:10	48n52
21:10–11	48n51
21:10—22:1	48
21:11	48n52
21:12	48n52
21:13	48n52
21:31—22:1	49n53
22	12
22:1	5, 46, 47, 47n47, 48, 48n51, 48n52, 49
22:1–20	91n81
22:1b	3n4
22:2	2n2, 5, 44n43, 46, 47, 47n47, 47n49, 48, 49, 59, 73, 74, 86, 88n79, 92
22:2–6	92–93
22:2–20	xvii, xix, 2, 21
22:2–21	xxiv, 1, 9, 13, 16, 17, 59n55, 74, 92, 114, 116, 117, 117n3, 118, 123, 125, 129
22:2—23:9	48
22:2—24:2	74
22:2—24:25	49–58, 49n54, 58–69, 99
22:2—25:9	48
22:3	49, 59
22:3a	5
22:3b	5
22:4	5, 49, 59
22:5	49, 59
22:6	50, 59, 71, 79, 80, 81, 103, 127
22:7	5, 50, 59
22:7–14b	93–95
22:7a	5
22:8	50, 59, 77, 79, 93
22:9	50, 59
22:10	50, 59
22:11	2n3, 50, 59–60, 71, 80, 94, 109
22:12	11n36, 50, 60, 76, 79, 80, 94, 109, 117n3, 119
22:13	50, 60
22:14	50, 60
22:14c–21	95–96
22:15	50, 60
22:15–17	84
22:15–40	84
22:16	51, 60
22:16–18	11
22:17	51, 60, 71, 80, 95, 110
22:18	11, 12n42, 43, 51, 60, 78, 95, 115, 116
22:19	2n3, 51, 60, 71, 84, 110, 115
22:19b	79
22:20	11n36, 43, 51, 60, 76, 78, 84, 96, 116, 117n3, 119, 120, 128n6
22:21	37n36, 51, 61, 84
22:21–35	xvii, xix, 2, 3, 21, 62n61
22:21–35a	5
22:21–40	91n81
22:22	37n36, 51, 61, 117n3
22:22–30	97
22:22–35	1, 9, 13, 16, 17, 18, 37n36, 74, 74n73, 116
22:22–40	xxiv, 59n55, 85n77, 96, 114, 116, 117, 118, 123, 125, 129
22:23	51, 61, 73, 86, 97
22:24	51, 61
22–24	xvii, xix, xx, xxii, xxiii, xxiv, 1, xviin1, 2, 2n3, 3, 5, 6, 6n19, 8, 9, 10, 12, 14, 15, 16, 17, 20, 21, 22, 23, 24, 25, 26,

Scripture Index

	27n15, 30, 33n29, 40, 41, 43, 44, 45, 46, 47, 48, 69–91, 83n77, 91n81, 92, 104, 106, 113, 114, 115, 116, 116n2, 123, 125, 129	23–4b	5
		23:5	53, 64–65, 78, 85
		23:6	53, 65
		23:7	54, 65, 80, 100, 110
		23:7–10	16n65, 85
		23:7b–10	72
		23:8	54, 65, 71, 80, 81, 100, 110, 127n4
22:25	51, 61, 73, 86, 97		
22:26	51–52, 61	23:9	54, 65, 71, 73, 75, 86, 100
22:27	52, 61, 73, 86, 97		
22:28	52, 61	23:10	47n49, 54, 65, 71, 81, 82, 100, 127n4
22:29	52, 61–62, 81		
22:30	52, 62, 62n61, 90	23:10—24:25	48
22:31	37n36, 52, 62, 62n61, 73, 75, 77, 84, 86, 98	23:11	54, 65, 79, 80, 100, 110
		23:12	43, 54, 65, 78, 85, 100, 116, 120
22:31–34	11n36		
22:31–35	98–99	23:13	54, 65, 74, 80, 86, 101, 102, 109
22:32	52, 62		
22:32–33	84	23:13–26	101–2
22:33	52, 62, 73, 81, 86, 98	23:14	54, 65, 82, 85, 102
		23:15	54, 65
22:34	52, 62–63, 84	23:16	54–55, 65–66, 78, 85
22:35	11n36, 43, 52, 63, 78, 84, 98, 116, 117n3, 128n6		
		23:17	55, 66
		23:18	55, 66
22:36	53, 63	23:18–24	16n65, 85
22:36–40	74n73, 99–100	23:18b–24	72
22:37	11, 53, 63	23:19	55, 66, 71, 95n83, 117
22:38	12n42, 43, 53, 63, 78, 89n80, 99, 116, 120, 128n6		
		23:20	55, 66, 71, 79, 102, 109, 117
22:39	53, 63	23:21	55, 66, 71, 74, 75, 86, 101, 102, 127n4
22:40	53, 63, 81, 82, 99		
22:41	44n43, 53, 63, 64n69, 71, 73, 85, 86, 100	23:22	55, 66, 71
		23:23	55, 66, 71
		23–24	12
22:41—23:12	100–101	23:24	55, 66, 71
22:41—23:26	3	23:25	55, 66, 79, 80, 102, 109
22:41—24:25	59n55, 74, 74n73, 91n81, 100		
		23:26	43, 55, 66, 78, 85, 102, 116, 120
23:1	53, 64		
23:2	53, 64, 81, 82, 85, 100	23:27	56, 67, 80, 103, 109
		23:27—24:25	103–4
23:3	2n3, 53, 64, 73, 78, 86, 100	23:28	56, 67, 76, 87, 103
		23:28—24:19	3
23:4	53, 64, 81, 82, 100	23:29	56, 67

139

Scripture Index

Numbers (*continued*)

23:30	56, 67, 82, 85, 103
24:1	2n3, 56, 67, 74, 87, 103, 109
24:2	56, 67, 74, 85, 87, 103
24:3	56, 67, 76, 87, 103
24:3–4	103
24:3–9	85
24:3b–9	72
24:4	56, 67, 71, 76, 77, 87, 103
24:5	56, 67, 71
24:5–9	85
24:6	56, 67–68, 71
24:7	56, 68, 71
24:8	56–57, 68, 71
24:9	57, 68, 71, 79, 80, 103, 104, 109, 127, 127n4
24:10	57, 68, 79, 80, 103, 109
24:11	57, 68, 71
24:11–14	11
24:12	57, 68
24:12–13	85
24:13	43, 57, 68, 71, 78, 103, 116, 120
24:14	43, 57, 68, 71
24:14b–24	5
24:15	57, 68, 76, 87, 103
24:15–16	103
24:15–19	85
24:15b–19	72
24:16	57, 68, 71, 76, 87, 103
24:17	57, 68–69, 71, 74, 76, 87, 103, 127n4
24:17–19	85
24:18	57–58, 69, 71
24:19	58, 69, 71
24:20	58, 69, 74, 87, 103
24:20–24	85
24:20b	72
24:21	58, 69, 74, 87, 103
24:21b–22	72
24:22	58, 69, 71
24:23	58, 69
24:23b–24	72
24:24	58, 69, 71
24:25	48, 49, 58, 69
25:1	47n49, 49
25:10	47n49
26:52	47n49
27	xix
27:15	47n49
28:26	47n49
30:2	47n49
31	10, 10n28
31:1	47n49
31:8	5, 10n28
31:16	10, 10n28
31:25	47n49
32:1	47n49
33:1	47n49
33:5–37	48n52, 49n52
33:41–48	48n52, 49n52
34:1	47n49
35:9	47n49
36	xix

Deuteronomy

12:15	83n76
12:21	83n76
13:15	82n76
23:3–6	10, 10n28

Joshua

13:22	10n28
24:9–10	10, 10n28

Judges

10:6—12:7	44
20:25, 35	39
20:35	39

Ruth

1–4	44

1 Samuel

28:24	83n76

Scripture Index

2 Samuel

11:1	39
11:1—12:25	39
11:1b	39
11:1c	39
11:15	39
11:17	39
11:21	39
11:24	39
11:26	39
12:5	39
12:13	39
12:14	39
12:18	39
12:19	39
12:21	39
12:23	39

1 Kings

19:21	83n76

Nehemiah

13:1–2	10n28
13:2	10

Isaiah

1:1	67n72

Ezekiel

12:27	67n72
34:3	83n76

Micah

6:5	10, 10n28

Ancient Near Eastern Texts

Balaam Bar Beor	14

Deir 'Allā inscription

DAT I:1–7	6n20
DAT II	6, 6n20, 8–9, 20

Dead Sea Scrolls

4Q23 Leviticus–Numbers^a	2n3
4Q27 Numbers^b	2n3
4Qnumb	2n3, 3n3

New Testament

2 Peter

2:15	10
2:15–16	10, 10n28

Jude

11	10, 10n28

Revelation

2:14	10, 10n28

www.ingramcontent.com/pod-product-compliance
Lightning Source LLC
Chambersburg PA
CBHW051107160426
43193CB00010B/1348